Samuel Henry Putnam

The story of Company A

Samuel Henry Putnam

The story of Company A

ISBN/EAN: 9783744749152

Printed in Europe, USA, Canada, Australia, Japan

Cover: Foto ©ninafisch / pixelio.de

More available books at **www.hansebooks.com**

THE STORY

OF

COMPANY A,

TWENTY-FIFTH REGIMENT, MASS. VOLS.,

IN THE

WAR OF THE REBELLION.

By SAMUEL H. PUTNAM.

WORCESTER, MASS.:
PUTNAM, DAVIS AND COMPANY, PUBLISHERS.
1886.

TO THE MEMORY

OF

𝕱𝖍𝖊 𝕯𝖊𝖆𝖉 𝖔𝖋 𝕮𝖔𝖒𝖕𝖆𝖓𝖞 𝕬,

I Dedicate

THIS SIMPLE STORY.

S. H. P.

Preface.

THIS STORY is written from the standpoint of a private soldier, for soldiers—the surviving members of Company A. It is an attempt to give, somewhat in detail, the everyday life of soldiers in active service and under canvas walls, with incidents of camp, march, and bivouac. The "Story" may possess but little merit, yet it may please the "Boys" for whom it was written.

No march is described in which the writer did not participate, no battle in which he did not take a hand, in his humble position; and it is claimed that the story is a true one. The language is sometimes rough, but it should be remembered that it was a rough life we were leading. If an occasional strong expression is found in these pages I can only say that "our army swore terribly in Flanders"; and I have tried to describe the soldier as I saw him —as I knew him.

I am indebted to my friend, Franklin P. Rice, for the elegant typographical appearance of the book. It is issued from his private press, and is entirely the work of his own hands. Thanks are due

Preface.

W. P. Derby, Esq., author of the History of the Twenty-seventh (Mass.) Regiment, for the use of the maps contained in this volume. The fine portrait of our Captain is from a photograph by Black of Boston, taken in 1863.

SAMUEL H. PUTNAM.

Worcester, Mass.
18th Annual Reunion of Co. A.,
    June 3d, 1886.

Contents.

CHAPTER I. FORMATION. Pages 7 to 22.

CHAPTER II. AT CAMP LINCOLN. Pages 23 to 35.

CHAPTER III. CAMP HICKS. Pages 36 to 45.

CHAPTER IV. THE BURNSIDE EXPEDITION. Pages 46 to 61.

CHAPTER V. THE BATTLE OF ROANOKE. Pages 62 to 96.

CHAPTER VI. THE CAPTURE OF NEW BERNE. Pages 97 to 111.

CHAPTER VII. NEW BERNE AND CAMP OLIVER. Pages 112 to 129.

CHAPTER VIII. EXPEDITIONS. Pages 130 to 158.

CHAPTER IX. EXPEDITIONS (*continued*). Pages 159 to 195.

CHAPTER X. CAMP, MARCH, AND BIVOUAC. Pages 196 to 226.

CHAPTER XI. RE-ENLISTING. Pages 227 to 256.

CHAPTER XII. THE BATTLE SUMMER. Pages 257 to 324.

Battles and Skirmishes

in which Company A took part.

ROANOKE ISLAND,	February 8, 1862.
NEW BERNE,	March 14, "
KINSTON,	December 14, "
WHITEHALL,	" 16, "
GOLDSBORO',	" 18, "
Near KINSTON,	March 6, 1863.
DEEP GULLY,	" 13, "
GUM SWAMP,	May 22, "
PORT WALTHAL,	" 6, 1864.
CHESTERFIELD JUNCTION,	" 7, "
ARROWFIELD CHURCH,	" 9, "
PALMER'S CREEK,	" 15, "
DREWRY'S BLUFF,	" 16, "
COBB'S HILL,	" 21, "
COLD HARBOR,	June 1, "
" "	" 2, "
" " Charge,	" 3, "
PETERSBURG, Guns captured,	" 15, "
"	" 16, "
" Charge,	" 18, "
"	" 30, "
" Crater,	July 30, "

THE STORY OF COMPANY A.

CHAPTER I.

FORMATION.

THE DARK CLOUDS which had so long lowered above the American horizon at last burst over the fiery land of South Carolina; and with the first gun fired by rebellious hands at Fort Sumter, the country was plunged into a whirlwind of civil war. <small>1861. *Opening of the Rebellion.*</small>

If, as Emerson says, the first shot fired at Concord was heard round the world, so the first shot at Sumter, April 12th, 1861, was not only heard round the world, but its echoes will resound through the ages; and the state which has the credit of commencing the fierce and bloody struggle of 1861,—that dastardly attempt to overthrow the freest and best government the world has ever seen—cannot escape being damned to an infamy for which history has no parallel.

1861. The election of Abraham Lincoln as President of the United States in 1860, was the signal for an uprising of the whole Slave Power against the prevailing free-labor sentiment of the Northern People. The conflict was inevitable, and while the South was organizing and arming, the North, depending upon the ability of the Government to protect itself, was in a measure unprepared for the terrible and bloody struggle that was soon to follow.

Massachusetts ready. Massachusetts, however, always watchful for the cause of Union and Liberty, was ready to meet the enemy when its uplifted hand should strike the blow. Governor John A. Andrew, foreseeing the approaching storm, wisely provided for the emergency; and by the promulgation of General Order *General Order No. 4.* No. 4, in January, 1861, the number of officers and men of the volunteer militia, who would respond instantly to any call which might be made upon them by the President of the United States, was ascertained with absolute accuracy.

The Worcester companies, City Guards and Light Infantry, voted almost unanimously "ready," as did most of the companies in the state. Subsequent events proved the wisdom of this order, for almost before the sound of the first hostile gun ceased its reverberations, the militia of the Old Commonwealth were marching to the relief of our defenseless Capital.

1861.

The men of Worcester, whose patriotism never failed, were among the first to answer the call to arms. The Sixth Regiment, with our Worcester Light Infantry, encountering armed treason in the streets of Baltimore, gallantly fought their way through to the city of Washington; and the ring of their muskets on the marble floor of the Senate Chamber gave assurance that the Capital was safe, and that the conspirators were foiled.

The Capital saved.

The Third Battalion Rifles, with the Worcester City Guards, Emmet Guards, and Holden Rifles, three full companies, proceeding to Annapolis, Md., and from thence to Fort McHenry, re-enforcing the handful of regulars there, saved that important position from capture by the secessionists of Baltimore. The Fourth, Fifth and Eighth regiments did excellent service at Fortress Monroe, the Relay House, and in Virginia.

Three Months' Men.

The State of Massachusetts had ever been noted for its excellent militia system, which in point of numbers and efficiency, was superior to all others. There were many people, however, who considered

The Militia.

<small>1861.</small> it useless and unprofitable. This sentiment was changed quite rapidly when the danger signal was sounded; and its enemies became its most enthusiastic friends when they found that these "holiday soldiers" were ready at a moment's notice to leave home, friends, business, *everything,*—going to scenes of strife and unknown dangers, perhaps never to return; but resolved to perform their duty to the country as soldiers and citizens, regardless of con-
<small>Its efficiency vindicated.</small> sequences to themselves. The three months' men, by their courage and devotion to duty in the hour of peril, checked the tide of treason, and proved the sterling worth of our volunteer militia. Their record is one which will ever redound to the glory of Massachusetts, and will be prized among her richest historic treasures.

<small>Second call for Troops.</small> On the 3d day of May, the President issued a proclamation calling for a force of volunteers to serve three years. He appealed to all loyal people to aid in maintaining the nation's honor and integrity. On the 15th of June, the first three years' regiment left the state, and others followed in rapid succession; the Fifteenth left Worcester on the 8th, and the Twenty-first on the 22nd of August.

The return of the Sixth Regiment and Third Battalion, August 2nd, after three months' service, was an occasion for general rejoicing. They were given a perfect ovation by the throngs of people that impeded their progress through the streets, with such demonstrations of welcome as had never been seen in Worcester before. The boys were glad enough to get home, but soon became restless, and nearly all of them re-entered the service, a large number as officers in the three years' regiments.

The public excitement at this time was intense. The people were thoroughly aroused. Thousands of loyal, patriotic men, regardless of politics or nationality, were seeking an opportunity to march to their imperilled country's defense. They had resolved to maintain the honor of the flag and the unity of the states at all hazards. They only desired leaders of ability and courage in whom they could place confidence. Officers of experience were in demand, and among those whose services were eagerly sought for was Lieut. Pickett of the Worcester City Guards. Previous to the war he had seen considerable service in the militia, joining Company F, Old Sixth Massachusetts, as early as 1840, and the Worcester City Guards in 1855. When the first call

1861.
Return of the Old Sixth.

Lieut. Pickett.

—— came, in April, 1861, he held a commission as lieutenant in this company. His ready and patriotic response, while others were hesitating, had made him conspicuous, and gave him a high reputation as a soldier of unquestioned ability and courage. Since his return from the three months' service, he had been offered the command of the Webster company in the Fifteenth, and the Barre company in the Twenty-first, but declined, preferring to remain with his old associates of the Third Battalion, who were arranging for the formation of a new regiment. The plan soon developed, and resulted in an order from Gov. Andrew, issued Sept. 10th, for the organization of a Worcester County regiment to be designated the Twenty-fifth; and Captain Josiah Pickett was authorized to recruit COMPANY A for this regiment. Headquarters were immediately opened at Brinley Hall, then the armory of the Guards, and business became brisk at once. The best young men in the city were eager to enlist in the new company under its popular commander, and quite a number of his old comrades in Company A, Third Rifles, were among the first to enroll themselves.

In ten days' time the ranks of the Company were filled with resolute, courageous young men, and it was waiting orders. On September 26th, orders were received to go into camp, and at 10 A. M. the same day, the company assembled for the last time in Brinley (now Grand Army) Hall, marched to the Agricultural Grounds, and went into camp, which was known as "Camp Lincoln." These grounds had a half-mile race track in the center, and ample sheds for cattle and horses on exhibition days, with a large building containing halls for the display of fruit, vegetables, and all farm products. The whole was enclosed with a high board fence, inside of which the soldiers were posted on guard duty, and paced their rounds with all the precision of regulars. These grounds, which were considered the largest in Massachusetts, were bounded on the east by what is now Sever street, on the north by Highland street, on the west by Agricultural street, and extended southerly nearly to Cedar street.

1861.

Camp Lincoln.

The organization of the Company was here completed. Francis E. Goodwin, a young business man of high character and patriotic purpose, and an old member of the City Guards, was appointed first lieutenant. Merrit B. Bessey, who had served with much credit in Company A, Third Rifles, in the three months' service, received the appointment of second

Company organized.

The Story of Company A.

<small>1861.</small> —— lieutenant; and the following is the full roster and roll of the Company:

<small>Roster.</small>

Name.	Rank.	Age.	Residence.
Josiah Pickett,	Captain,	38	Worcester.
Francis E. Goodwin,	1st Lieut.,	31	" "
Merrit B. Bessey,	2d "	22	" "
George A. Johnson,	1st Sergt.,	42	" "
George Burr,	Sergt.,	26	" "
James M. Hervey,	"	23	" "
James J. McLane,	"	24	" "
Welcome W. Sprague,	"	33	" "
Frank L. R. Coes,	Corp.,	23	" "
Jaalam Gates,	"	38	" "
Calvin A. Wesson,	"	29	Grafton.
Edwin A. Morse,	"	19	Worcester.
Henry M. Ide,	"	30	" "
John A. Thompson,	"	22	" "
John A. Chenery,	"	26	" "
Samuel H. Putnam,	"	27	" "
Jubal H. Haven,	Musician,	54	" "
Jesse L. Yeaw,	"	19	Northboro'.
Sylvanus G. Bullock,	Wagoner,	27	Worcester.
Nathaniel O. Adams,	Private,	23	Boston.
Samuel C. T. Aborn,	"	27	Worcester.
Charles S. Bartlett,	"	19	" "

25th Regt., Mass. Vols.

Name.	Rank.	Age.	Residence.	
George R. Brown,	Private,	23	Grafton.	1861.
Moses P. Brown,	" "	21	Worcester.	*Roll of the Company.*
Moses L. Bolster, Jr.,	" "	20	" "	
Francis B. Brock,	" "	28	Athol.	
Henry D. Brock,	" "	19	" "	
Hamlin Butterfield,	" "	21	Sterling.	
Horace E. Brooks,	" "	26	Worcester.	
David B. Bigelow,	" "	29	" "	
George W. Bigelow,	" "	18	" "	
Albert N. Bonn,	" "	24	" " [Ct.	
Cyrus Brumley,	" "	24	Jewett City,	
Hiram H. H. Billings,	" "	25	Worcester.	
George E. Curtis,	" "	21	" "	
Samuel S. Dresser,	" "	20	" "	
Reuben H. DeLuce,	" "	22	Boston.	
Thomas Earle,	" "	38	Worcester.	
Lewis J. Elwell,	" "	18	" "	
Joseph P. Eaton,	" "	21	Auburn.	
Daniel T. Eaton,	" "	31	" "	
Elbridge B. Fairbanks,	" "	30	Worcester.	
Jerome H. Fuller,	" "	18	" "	
Charles Forbes,	" "	42	" "	
Francis Greenwood,	" "	22	" "	
John L. Goodwin,	" "	20	" "	

1861.
Roll of the Company.

Name.	Rank.	Age.	Residence.
Henry Goulding, 2d,	Private,	30	Worcester.
James M. Green,	" "	21	Boston.
Andrew L. George,	" "	21	Worcester.
Charles Henry,	" "	44	" "
Cyrus L. Hutchins,	" "	30	" "
Edward S. Hewitt,	" "	21	Auburn.
John W. Hartshorn,	" "	22	Worcester.
William E. Holman,	" "	19	" "
Cyrus W. Holman,	" "	21	" "
Edward P. Hall,	" "	19	" "
William R. Keef,	" "	20	Auburn.
Charles H. Knowlton,	" "	23	Worcester.
Benjamin C. Knowles,	" "	42	Auburn.
Augustus Knowles,	" "	21	" "
Lucius F. Kingman,	" "	19	Northboro'.
Henry F. Knox,	" "	28	Holden.
Walter D. Knox,	" "	22	" "
William L. Lyon,	" "	20	Worcester.
Charles A. Mayers,	" "	20	Auburn.
Charles H. Monroe,	" "	20	Worcester.
Lloyd G. Manning,	" "	23	" "
George E. Merrill,	" "	23	" "
Daniel M. G. Merrill,	" "	26	" "
Charles Matherson,	" "	25	Boston.

25th Regt., Mass. Vols.

Name.	Rank.	Age.	Residence.	
Chauncey L. Metcalf,	Private,	36	Worcester.	1861.
Eli Pike,	" "	19	" "	Roll
George F. Penniman,	" "	22	" "	of the
Sidney W. Phillips,	" "	24	" "	Company.
Henry H. Pratt,	" "	21	Grafton.	
William W. Putnam,	" "	21	" "	
Orrin Parsons,	" "	34	Worcester.	
Walter H. Richards,	" "	18	" "	
George F. Robinson,	" "	21	" "	
Henry W. Reed,	" "	18	" "	
Amos E. Stearns,	" "	28	" "	
George F. Stearns,	" "	22	Clinton.	
John B. Savage,	" "	25	Worcester.	
George L, Seagrave,	" "	24	Uxbridge.	
Hiram Staples,	" "	20	Douglas.	
Elijah Simonds,	" "	39	Worcester.	
Charles Smith,	" "	39	" "	
Paris Smith,	" "	44	" "	
Augustus Stone,	" "	20	" "	
Julius M. Tucker,	" "	20	" "	
Nelson Tiffany,	" "	18	Auburn.	
Chester O. Upham,	" "	35	Worcester.	
Alonzo D. Whitcomb,	" "	26	" "	
Frederick A. White,	" "	20	" "	

The Story of Company A.

	Name.	Rank.	Age.	Residence.
1861.	Hale Wesson,	Private,	19	Grafton.
Roll of the Company.	James Wesson,	" "	18	" "
	Frank Wright,	" "	20	Holden.
	John Wright,	" "	18	Worcester.
	Edwin D. Waters,	" "	25	Millbury.
	Timothy M. Ward,	" "	19	Worcester.
	Cyrus K. Webber,	" "	20	Brookfield.

Total : officers, 3 ; men, 98 = 101.

NAMES OF RECRUITS.

	Name.	Rank.	Age.	Residence.
	Abel S. Angell,	Private,	18	Boston.
Names of recruits.	Sidney J. Atkinson,	" "	42	Worcester.
	Charles E. Benson,	" "	20	Blackstone.
	Walter S. Bugbee,	" "	30	Worcester.
	Daniel W. Burt,	" "	24	" "
	John P. Coulter,	" "	19	Clinton.
	Charles A. Davis,	" "	18	Upton.
	Joseph L. Delaney,	" "	33	Auburn.
	Horace W. Dryden,	" "	23	Worcester.
	Charles Eaton,	" "	22	Gardner.
	Timothy Foley,	" "	19	Worcester.
	Benjamin C. Green,	" "	25	" "
	Reuben Heywood,	" "	21	" "
	Charles B. Kendall,	" "	21	" "

25th Regt., Mass. Vols.

Name.	Rank.	Age.	Residence.	
James Kerwin,	Private,	44	Worcester.	1861.
William R. Leseur,	" "	19	Milford.	*Names of recruits.*
Horace Lincoln,	" "	26	Charlestown.	
Ira Lindsey,	" "	38	Worcester.	
John Madden,	" "	44	" "	
Andrew J. McKinstry,	" "	44	Southbridge.	
Bernard McSheny,	" "	36	Mendon.	
John Moore,	" "	18	Dudley.	
George H. Nottage,	" "	18	Hopkinton.	
Charles O'Neil,	" "	18	Milford.	
George Packard,	" "	24	Fitchburg.	
Henry A. Pond,	" "	18	Milford.	
Lyman J. Prentiss,	" "	21	Northbridge.	
Charles D. Roby,	" "	19	Worcester.	
Edward J. Sargent,	" "	21	Oakham.	
George E. Sawyer,	" "	23	Clinton.	
Liberty W. Stone,	" "	38	Milford.	
James D. Thompson,	" "	21	Oxford.	
Joseph H. Thompson,	" "	19	Worcester.	
Charles E. Wheeler,	" "	39	Uxbridge.	
James White,	" "	45	Worcester.	
George W. Wood,	" "	18	Upton.	
William H. Wood,	" "	18	" "	

Number of Recruits, 37.

1861.

Colonel Upton.

The Twenty-fifth Regiment was a Worcester County regiment, nearly all of the officers and men belonging to that section. The commanding officer was Colonel Edwin Upton, of Fitchburg, forty-five years of age, firm and dignified in bearing, genial and courteous to every one. For many years connected with the Massachusetts Militia, he was a thorough soldier and a brave officer. Resigning on account of disability after more than a year's service, it is but little to say that he was beloved by every soldier in the Regiment. He still lives (April, 1886), a wreck of his former self, having lost his sight by a terrible accident while blasting rocks. Peace be with him. May his end be like the going down of the sun in a cloudless sky—calm, serene, and beautiful.

Lt.-Col. Sprague.

The Lieutenant-Colonel was A. B. R. Sprague, of slight build and gentlemanly appearance, thirty-four years of age, and a resident of Worcester. He, also, was a militia officer of years of experience, and served during the three months' campaign as Captain of Company A (City Guards), in the Third Battalion Rifles. He was thoroughly familiar with military tactics, and a strict disciplinarian. He resigned after about a year's service in the Twenty-fifth, and appeared again in the field as Colonel of the Fifty-first, a nine months' regiment; later he was Colonel of the Second Massachusetts Heavy Artillery, and was mustered out of the service in 1865 as Brevet Brigadier-General. He is, at present writing, living in Worcester, and is still on duty as Sheriff of the County.

1861.

Major Matthew J. McCafferty was thirty-two years old, and a resident of Worcester. He was one of the (very) few lawyers of Worcester who, in 1861, locked their office doors, threw away the keys, and fought under the starry folds of "Old Glory." He was also a three months' man, serving as Lieutenant in the Emmet Guards; and remained with the Twenty-fifth until after the battles of Roanoke and New Berne, when he returned home and effectively aided the cause by furthering enlistments, and delivering many patriotic addresses. At the time of his death, in May, 1885, he was one of the justices of the Boston Municipal Court.

Major McCafferty.

Our Adjutant was Elijah A. Harkness, twenty-three years old, and a man of very delicate build for a soldier. He resided in Worcester, and had served in the three months' campaign as Lieutenant in the City Guards. He resigned to accept the position

Adjutant Harkness.

1861.
—— of Major in the Fifty-first Regiment. After the war he went to Chicago, where he died.

Surgeon Rice.
The Surgeon was J. Marcus Rice, a well known physician of Worcester, thirty-four years old. He was wounded at Roanoke, was afterwards Medical Director of the Eighteenth Army Corps, and still later, Medical Inspector of the Army of the James, serving through the war. He is still in practice in Worcester, as genial and full of business as ever.

Chaplain James.
Our Chaplain was Rev. Horace James, Pastor of the Old South Church in Worcester. After the battle of New Berne he had charge of the freedmen, and was afterwards Captain and Assistant Quartermaster, U. S. Vols. He died in 1875.

Quartermaster Brown.
The Quartermaster, William O. Brown of Fitchburg, was forty-six years of age. He was a man— everybody liked him—always pleasant, and ever ready to do a good turn for the private soldier— no wonder everybody liked him. He served his full time of three years, and is now living in Fitchburg, holding the office of County Commissioner. Everybody likes him still.

Let us now glance at life in Camp Lincoln.

CHAPTER II.

AT CAMP LINCOLN.

THE MEMBERS of the Company, after selecting tent-mates, quickly adapted themselves to the routine of camp life. The work of drill and discipline now began in earnest. The nucleus of old soldiers in the ranks of the Company was of great advantage; as instructors to the new men they were invaluable. This was soon manifested in the excellent appearance of the Company on drill or parade. Company A was assigned the post of honor on the right of the regimental line.

It was interesting to witness the change from citizens to soldiers. Camp life was new to the majority of the Company, but after a few days of the regular company drill, and a few nights of sleeping in tents, the novelty wore off; and when the time came to break camp, it was hard to distinguish the three months men from those of less experience.

1861.

Adaptation to Camp Life.

Company A, being the right flank company, was drilled in the bayonet exercise, and also the skirmish drill. These evolutions always attracted a crowd of spectators from the numbers which thronged the grounds, and were performed with the greatest enthusiasm by the Company daily. As to amusements while in Camp Lincoln, it must be confessed that the crowds of visitors were so great that there was little time to attend to any; still athletic exercises were indulged in to some extent. Boxing, gymnastics, and running races around the half-mile track were daily practiced. The weather was delightful during the stay of the Twenty-fifth at Camp Lincoln; and although the nights were often cold and frosty, the days were clear and bright. The recollection of those crisp, sparkling October days of 1861 comes back to us like the memory of a pleasant dream.

The tents used by the Company in Camp Lincoln were A tents, and were intended to hold six men each, with all their equipments. This was rather crowding things, and a good deal like packing sardines in a box; still it was taken as a matter of course, and the inconvenience submitted to in perfect good nature. These tents were, some time after, exchanged for Sibley tents,—much more comfortable

—later for shelter tents, and at last, while before Petersburg, for no tents at all.

1861.

The streets in Camp Lincoln were named. Our company street was designated, as the signboard read, "Pickett Avenue," in honor of our Captain. The tents bore names according to the whims of the occupants. One was known as "Rovers' Lodge," another as "Whispering House," probably because it was the noisiest tent on the street. There were "Upton's Hotel," "Orphans' Home" and others. These were amusing to visitors and created a deal of merriment as they read the names. So with drilling four or five hours daily, guard mounting, dress parade, inspection, and crowds of visitors, the days passed rapidly away.

Camp Names.

On the 17th of October we were mustered into the service of the United States by Captain J. M. Goodhue, and were citizens no longer. Clothing was served out to us at this time, and bidding adieu to citizens' attire for three years, we were arrayed in the blue of Uncle Sam; and with the ungainly black regulation hat, and clumsy overcoat and brogans, the transformation from citizens to soldiers was complete. The brogans caused a deal of fun among the boys, and some were loth to give up the nice-

Muster in.

1861. — fitting civilian's boot, and tried to fight it out on that line; but the brogan conquered, and it was found by experience that the army shoe with its wide sole, and its broad, low heel, was the best thing for marching. Our rifles were soon after received, and we now fancied ourselves soldiers indeed.

Clothing of the Soldier. Each soldier was entitled to clothing as follows: One dress (frock) coat of dark blue cloth, with brass buttons; one fatigue jacket, dark blue, coarser cloth, brass buttons; pants and overcoat of light blue; woolen shirts and drawers, blue-mixed or gray; solid sewed brogans tied with leather strings; and finally the broad-brimmed black felt hat, turned up on the left with a brass eagle to fasten it in that position; and the blue cap with a broad visor, with the number of the regiment and the letter of the company on the crown, which sloped towards the visor. Such was the clothing of the soldier of 1861 at Camp Lincoln. He also drew a large, brown U. S. blanket and a rubber blanket.

In his every-day or working dress while in Camp Lincoln, our soldier wore his blue jacket with brass buttons, his pants of light blue, and cap with broad visor; and with his woolen shirt, drawers, stockings and brogans, he was, if not a handsome, at least a comfortable looking soldier. At dress parade, inspections and reviews, he wore his blue dress coat, and the ugly black felt hat turned up at the side, instead of the blue jacket and fatigue cap. *1861.*

This is, as we call him up from memory, the way our Company A soldier was dressed at Camp Lincoln. As we stood in line in heavy marching order, we were dressed in our best, with equipments on, rifles to the shoulder, and knapsacks on our backs.* The knapsack contained all we possessed in the way of extra clothing, and the overcoat, while in a neat roll on its top was the woolen blanket with the rubber blanket outside. The haversack contained a tin plate, knife, fork, spoon, and a tin cup holding a quart. The canteen filled with water was indispensable. Now, for the moment, if we look at him three years later, we shall find something of a change in his appearance. He is in the trenches before Petersburg during that terrible summer of 1864. His knapsack is gone—they were all stored in Portsmouth during the Petersburg campaign. The ugly black hat with its brass eagle has disappeared; that vanished in Carolina long ago. Over- *In Marching Order.* *Three Years later.*

---

*The total weight of arms, equipments and extra clothing carried by each soldier was about forty-five pounds. It is safe to say that the knapsacks were never again loaded so heavily as at this time.

1861. coats have nearly all departed, and very few have woolen blankets. Thus we see the veteran stripped to the very lightest possible fighting trim ; the clothes which he has on, his equipments, his trusty old Enfield rifle, his haversack containing plate and other utensils, canteen and rubber blanket, are all that he carries with him. The last is rolled lengthwise and thrown over the neck like a horse collar, with the ends tied together hanging down the left side. The woolen blanket, if he possessed one, was rolled within the other. That is all that is left of our soldier now. Tents there are none ; he sleeps on the ground in the open air. His comrades are many of them dead, in rebel prisons, sick, and scattered far away—but I anticipate.

Preparations for Departure. On the 21st of October the regimental baggage wagons arrived, twelve in all, besides the hospital teams, and the lonesome looking ambulances. On the 30th, the Regiment was reviewed by Governor Andrew and staff, the grounds being crowded with spectators. The Governor made a stirring address to the soldiers, and complimented the Regiment on its fine and soldierly appearance.

On the 31st of October orders were given to break camp. Now all was excitement ; the packing of knapsacks—and they were never so solidly packed again; orders quickly given and as quickly obeyed; the hum of hurried conversation, and bursts of laughter from the different tents—all denoted that we were to move. A collation provided by Worcester ladies was served in the Hall, a good part of the *rations* which were on the tables quietly finding a place in the haversacks of the soldiers. Rations? —army rations?—nay, verily; generous, kind, too kind, friends of the soldiers allowed us to eat very little of army rations while at Camp Lincoln. Indeed, it seemed as if we had everything but army rations. It was a different story a few days after— nothing but army rations then. Pies, cakes, butter, and all the various knicknacks of civilized cookery vanished, and the substantial salt horse and hard tack came to the front, and came to stay. After all, the ordinary bill of fare of the private soldier, compared with that of his civilized friends, was the healthier of the two.

The men were now placed in position around their respective tents; at a given signal every tent fell as if by magic, and Camp Lincoln was numbered among the things that were. Regimental line was formed about three o'clock, and as we stood there in heavy

1861.

Rations in Camp Lincoln.

1861. — marching order, it certainly appeared more like business; and it seemed hardly possible that these men, tanned by a month's exposure to the open air, could be the same pale-faced ones who first appeared in citizens' dress at Camp Lincoln.

March through the City. Passing out of the western gate, the principal entrance to the grounds, we moved through Agricultural and Highland streets, and wheeling into Main street, marched company front to the Common, where the train was waiting for us on the Norwich railroad. The most intense excitement prevailed throughout the city. Such crowds of people filled the streets as to impede the march of the Regiment; every window had its anxious interested faces; roofs of buildings were crowded with excited men; cheers from the crowds responded to with cheers from the Regiment; the waving of handkerchiefs and flags; and the stirring strains of the Regimental Band — all tended to make it one of the most exciting scenes we had ever witnessed.

Oct. 31. *Departure.* At 4 P. M., the train was in motion, and amid deafening cheers and fluttering of handkerchiefs, moved rapidly off. Fainter grew the cheering and soon died away; and the soldiers, excited as they were when they entered the cars, soon quieted down, and it was easy to see there were sober, earnest, thoughtful faces among them. Where are we going? How many of us will return? Shall we find them all at home if we do return? These thoughts undoubtedly filled the minds of many of the boys as the train sped rapidly on, and the shades of night gathered around; and it is sad indeed to think after the lapse of so many years, how many of that thousand men did not return.

1861.
Sober Thoughts.

Allyn's Point was reached about 9, and soon after midnight the Regiment embarked on board the steamer *Connecticut* for New York. We had ample accomodations on the *floors* of the steamboat, and with our woolen blankets and overcoats were very comfortable. We had a quiet passage to New York, which place we reached about nine o'clock on the morning of November 1. Marching down Broadway, company front, sweeping the street from sidewalk to sidewalk, band playing, and the whole Regiment singing "John Brown's body lies mouldering in the grave," we had another exciting scene before us. Broadway, always a crowded thoroughfare, was literally packed with people, and the Regiment was received with the greatest enthusiasm. Reaching the City Hall Park, we were provided with breakfast

New York City.

1861.

Park Barracks.

—— in the dingy-looking buildings known as the Park Barracks. · These rough buildings, dirty on the outside, had interiors repulsive, with anything but a pleasant air about them; and the breakfast was not of the most inviting character. Perhaps Massachusetts soldiers were a little particular, but that breakfast was untouched by many of Company A.

Philadelphia.

Cooper Shop.

Late in the afternoon we left the Park Barracks, and marching through crowded streets again to the ferry, were soon in Jersey City, and entering the cars went whirling away towards the Land of Brotherly Love. Philadelphia was reached about midnight, and what a surprise awaited us here. We were marched to the famous Cooper Shop, where thousands of soldiers passing through Philadelphia were fed weekly all through the war. What a contrast to the Park Barracks of New York City. Here was a large, brilliantly lighted hall, with long rows of tables loaded down with the greatest abundance of well-cooked food: tea, coffee, cold meats, bread and butter, pies, etc., that brought exclamations of delight from the hungry lips of the tired soldiers; and not only were the soldiers themselves filled, but many a haversack went from the Cooper Shop full to bursting. Neatly dressed, pleasant-faced young ladies and gentlemen were in attendance, and met with a smile the hurried questions of a crowd of rough soldiers. Wash basins with cool water and clean towels were plenty; and a thousand soldiers marched through Philadelphia that night breathing a thousand blessings on the Cooper Shop, its founder, and its genial, kind-hearted attendants.

1861.

In marching across the city to the Baltimore Depot, the regimental band-playing and the soldiers' singing awoke the echoes of the Quaker City, and many of its inhabitants. Windows were hastily thrown up as the Regiment passed, and cheers from the houses were drowned by rousing cheers from the soldiers. Handkerchiefs were waved, and often articles of white much larger than handkerchiefs were shaken from upper story windows. On the whole, the midnight march through Philadelphia was an enthusiastic one; and the Massachusetts soldiers felt like showering blessings on the inhabitants of the city of William Penn.

Midnight March.

In the early morning, about four o'clock, we were once more in the cars, pushing on towards Baltimore. It was nearly noon, November 2d, when the train reached Havre de Grace, and we were taken across the Susquehanna River on the huge ferry boat at that place. This boat took at one trip the whole train, with its passengers (one thousand soldiers) and all their traps. At this time it was raining hard, and the weather continued wet and unpleasant till Baltimore was reached. We found the railroad guarded by soldiers (the first we had seen on duty) from Havre de Grace to Baltimore, a picket guard being stationed at every bridge and crossing. Baltimore was reached about three in the afternoon, and in a driving rain we marched to the steamboat landing, and went on board the steamer *Louisiana*, expecting to sail at once; but for some reason we did not move until the next day, Company A being quartered on the steamer for the night.

Sunday morning at nine we sailed for Annapolis. We could see little of Baltimore from the steamer, save Federal Hill, which had been fortified, and was held by Duryea's Zouaves. We steamed along past Fort McHenry and Fort Carroll, where some of the Company A boys had been posted during the three months' service, and reached Annapolis about noon, marching directly to the Academy buildings near by. Here we found many friends, for the Twenty-first Massachusetts Regiment was on duty here, and we of the Twenty-fifth fared well at their hands.

Our Chaplain, Rev. Horace James, with Chaplain Ball of the Twenty-first, held religious services in the afternoon. The grounds belonging to the Naval Academy, though in a sad state of neglect at this time, were, when in order and properly cared for, very neat and attractive; but the Naval School had been removed to Newport, R. I., and the buildings were now used as barracks for soldiers.

On Monday, November 4th, we marched through the streets of Annapolis, about two miles from the place of landing, to a large, pleasant field on the farm of one Taylor, where our tents were pitched in regular form. This was our first camp since leaving Camp Lincoln, and we will defer our account of the incidents here to another chapter.

1861.

First Camp.

CHAPTER III.

CAMP HICKS.

1861.
Nov. 4.
Camp Hicks.

OUR CAMP at Annapolis was known as "Camp Hicks," from the loyal Governor of Maryland of that name. At this time the Fifty-first New York was the only regiment on the ground. Here we began to find out what army rations were, and everything was more like business. We drilled seven or eight hours daily, and Company A was worked hard as skirmishers, and in the bayonet exercise. We occupied the same A tents as at Camp Lincoln. Camp Hicks was very pleasantly situated, and fortunately we had good water—a very important item in camp life—which was obtained from a sort of ravine at the rear of the camp, through which flowed a small sluggish stream. A hole was dug in the ground, and a barrel with the ends knocked out sunk down into it; this furnished a supply for one company. We rigged up a well-sweep—a gentle reminder of New England—only in place of the "Old Oaken Bucket" we had an old iron kettle, which answered the same purpose. The first few days in Camp Hicks were rather tough for us; for some reason no straw had been obtained to sleep on, and although we spread our rubber blankets on the ground, and had woolen blankets and overcoats, still the rubber blanket, while it kept out the dampness, would not keep out the chill from the ground, which is as bad. The consequence was, very many of the boys caught severe colds and were coughing continually for some time after. It is a curious fact that, after these colds were gotten rid of, we seldom heard of such a thing as a cough in the Company during the whole time of service.

The first few days in Camp Hicks there appeared to be some trouble about the rations; and when, one day, we had raw salt pork and hard tack for dinner, with water to drink, and another day no dinner at all, we could not help longing for the Philadelphia Cooper Shop and its pleasant attendants. But all this was straightened out after a little time. We soon had plenty of straw for our beds, hot coffee and soft bread for breakfast and supper, and either salt beef or pork with beans, rice or potatoes for dinner, in abundance and nicely cooked. It was army rations now (except an occasional box from home), and henceforth to the end. Probably no soldiers in the world were ever so well provided for as were our men of the North during the Rebellion.

1861.

Speaking from experience as a private soldier in the ranks of Company A, I must say that the rations were excellent, and the clothing first-class. Whenever we drew any article of clothing not up to the mark, or anything in the way of rations that was not good, as wormy hard tack or poor salt beef, it was the rare exception, and not the rule by any means.

Quality of Supplies.

Life at Camp Hicks glided quietly away. We had enough to do, certainly, with six to eight hours drill daily, inspections, reviews, target shooting, &c.; but we found time to write, and time for amusements such as they were—card-playing and smoking, cribbage, reading and writing, covering about the whole ground; and a stroll through the camp at any hour of the day was sure to find more or less smoking, and in the evening after supper, card-playing and other indoor amusements were in order. It was a pleasing sight to look into one of the small A tents after nightfall, and see a bayonet stuck in the ground

Camp Life.

in the center, with a lighted candle inserted in the end, to light up the not over roomy canvas; and a merry group of half a dozen card players busy with their cards, and of course their pipes. What fun for them; hear them laugh and shout; now a song in which they all join, now a story. Thus they while the hours away.

The weather during November and December was very pleasant for the most part,—much like the October weather of New England; but it grew colder, and on the morning of December 3d we found the ground frozen quite hard, and water in pails outside the tents had frozen about half an inch. This set the boys to contriving ways to warm the tents, and after some experimenting they hit upon a plan something like this. A pit was dug in the center of the tent perhaps eighteen inches deep, and as large as could be nicely covered with a flat stone. This pit was sometimes lined with stones somewhat after the style of a well, to keep the earth from caving in. From the bottom of the pit a hole was dug to the outside of the tent, in front or to one side, for the entrance of fresh air; then from near the top of the pit a hole was made to the outside of the tent in the rear, as an outlet for the smoke; over this hole out-

1861.

First Cold Weather.

How the Tents were Warmed.

side a chimney was built of mud and sticks, or a barrel which answered as well, and the thing was complete. Now build a fire in the pit, cover the top with the flat stone, and the Lord willing, and the wind in the right direction, what smoke did not find its way into the tent might possibly go out of the chimney. This experiment was, perhaps, fairly successful, and some tents were made quite warm in this way.

1861.

The sergeants' tent was a regular officers' or wall tent, with a fly or large sheet of canvas drawn over the top, making a sort of double roof. This tent was occupied by the five sergeants of Company A, and the cook; and a right merry crowd it was. The first or orderly sergeant was George A. Johnson, a man over forty years of age, of soldierly bearing, dark complexion, black hair and full black beard streaked with gray, eyes black as midnight, well read, full of fun, and the best story-teller in the Twenty-fifth Regiment. "Old Posey" was his pet name. Connected with the militia many years, he was a thorough soldier, and served in the three months' campaign. He was promoted to a lieutenancy in the Twenty-fifth Regiment, was wounded at Cold Harbor, and after the war enlisted in the regular service, and was on

Sergeant Johnson.

duty on the northern frontier at the time of the Fenian raid in 1866. He died in 1881. We shall see him again before the story is told.

1861.

The second sergeant was George Burr,—"Birdie" we called him. Burr was the pony* sergeant of Company A. He was also a three months man, twenty-six years old, of pleasant, cheerful disposition, and a perfect pink of neatness—a gentleman as well as a soldier. He was promoted to a second lieutenancy, was wounded at Cold Harbor, and was mustered out at the end of the three years as first lieutenant in the Twenty-fifth. He is, at present writing, engaged in a successful business in Worcester, and is as cheerful and pleasant as ever.

Sergeant Burr.

The third sergeant was James J. McLane. Jimmy or "Jemsy," as we called him, was of Irish extraction, twenty-four years old, tall, straight as a ramrod, a splendid soldier and a genial, social comrade. He, too, served with credit in the three months' service, and was promoted to be lieutenant in a "Buffalo" regiment (North Carolina Union troops), where he achieved honor and a name; and was mustered out as captain in that regiment at the end of the war.

Sergeant McLane.

* "Pony," i. e. short in stature. The men at the left of the Company were of course the shortest, and hence "ponies."

1861. Jemsy is now, and has been for years, on the Worcester police force, and his tall form can be seen "on duty" any day in the streets of Worcester as he walks his beat.

Sergeant Sprague. The fourth sergeant was another three months man, Welcome W. Sprague. He was provost sergeant, and did not do duty with the Company. He was of a social nature, and could ill be spared from the merry ring of sergeants of Company A. He died in New York City in 1884.

Sergeant Putnam. Of the fifth sergeant at Camp Hicks it becometh me to say little. He was by name Samuel H. Putnam, by calling a clerk, with no knowledge whatever of military affairs at time of enlistment, but possibly an average soldier. It can be said of him that he was reliable ; and he was with Company A in all its wanderings, and one of the four out of the hundred men who started with the Company that went through all its marches and all its battles to the final muster out. After the war he engaged in business as bookseller, and has followed it in the same shop to the present time, a period of twenty years. We shall see him again.

The Cook. The cook was Charles Henry—"Uncle Henry" we called him—forty-four years old,—too old for a sol-

25th Regt., Mass. Vols. 43

dier. He was a heavy built man, dark and swarthy, rough spoken, but good hearted, and much liked by the men.

1861.

Life in the sergeants' tent at Camp Hicks was very pleasant. The tent was much larger than the A tent, and with the same number of men to occupy it, gave ample room for a table and seats, and also a stove, which as the weather grew colder, made cheerful and comfortable quarters. A dainty set of lads were the sergeants of Company A. They had a coffee pot of their own, and ye gods! what coffee came from that tin pot. Sergeant Sprague being provost sergeant was relieved from company duty, and it was for him to see that our breakfast was got up properly, and well he performed the service. Coffee always hot, bread toasted, good butter (not an army ration) that we bought, and other luxuries, —"who wouldn't be a soger?" Our stove worked admirably, and with plenty of blankets, table, stools, &c., the sergeants' tent of Company A was as complete and comfortable as the ingenuity of its occupants could make it.

Sergeants' Tent.

As time went on, Christmas, 1861, dawned on us still at Camp Hicks. Inspection in the forenoon, and a holiday in the afternoon. Cards and pipes

Christmas Day.

—— are in the ascendant to-day. It is plain to see that coffee, cards and tobacco are the three great essentials to a soldier's life.

1862. January.

A few days before Christmas we had a pay-day, at which *Greenbacks* made their first appearance; and *Gold* made its last appearance to the soldier in January, 1862.

First Greenbacks.

January 1, 1862, the New Year was ushered in by a snow squall. January 2d, at brigade drill, we had a sort of mimic battle, and Company A acted as skirmishers, using blank cartridges. The Company received some praise for its good work.

New Year.

On Saturday, January 4th, we received orders to strike tents Monday morning, so at six o'clock A. M. of that day, we turned out, and the tents were struck. It had snowed during the night, and the snow was still falling as the line was formed; it seemed quite like a New England winter morning. After firing a parting salute we marched away from Camp Hicks, which had been our home for two months. Reaching Annapolis we went, after much delay, on board the steamer *New York*. Company I, Capt. Parkhurst, went on board the schooner *Skirmisher;* companies D and H on board the gunboat *Zouave;* and the *New York* took the other seven companies

Jan. 6. Good bye to Camp Hicks.

of the Regiment. When all was ready on board the
New York, the steamer pushed out a mile or so into
the stream and came to anchor. We now had time
to look around us, and a busy scene it was to gaze
upon. The sleepy old town of Annapolis had not
seen so much life in a century. Large numbers of
vessels of all descriptions,—steamers, sailing craft,
tugboats, moving about in all directions; others at
the various landings, loading or unloading,—all combined to make a busy picture such as the old town
will not see for another century. This was the
preparation for the famous Burnside Expedition.

1862.

CHAPTER IV.

THE BURNSIDE EXPEDITION.

1862.
Jan. 9.
Sailing of the Burnside Expedition.

IT WAS NOT until about 8 A. M. of January 9th, 1862, that the Burnside Expedition finally left the old town of Annapolis, and moved grandly out into the waters of Chesapeake Bay, the steamer *New Brunswick*, with Gen. Foster and staff on board, taking the lead; the *New York*, with the Twenty-fifth Massachusetts, being second in line. Gen. Burnside modestly took the small steamer *Picket* for his headquarters. There were over one hundred vessels in the expedition, and a grander sight could hardly be imagined than was presented as it sailed away from Annapolis town. Numbers of the steamers had sailing vessels in tow, and the *New York* had an old canal boat towing astern, which bore the ominous name of *Bomb Shell*. It was one of the fairest of fair days, and with flags and streamers flying, bands playing, and soldiers cheering, it seemed more like a monster holiday excursion than the starting of a hostile expedition.

1862.

There had been, of course, much surmising about the destination of the expedition, and all sorts of guesses were made, but nothing definite was known in regard to it excepting that we were to rendezvous at Fortress Monroe. On the steamer *New York*, Company A occupied the upper cabin forward; the sergeants occupying a state room close by. The morning was rainy, but in the afternoon it cleared away and we had a good part of the fleet in sight, sailing in a long line, each vessel in its proper place. Evening came on clear and bright with a beautiful moonlight, but a heavy fog afterwards arose, and we came to anchor near the mouth of the Potomac and remained there all night.

The morning of January 10th opened heavy with fog, but it cleared up about nine, and we proceeded on our way. Soon Fortress Monroe was in sight, with a crowd of vessels; and as we came nearer we passed several American men of war, the *Minnesota*, *Jamestown*, *Roanoke*, and one Frenchman. The jolly tars greeted us with rousing cheers from the rigging of their vessels as we passed, to which we responded most heartily. About noon we anchored

Fortress Monroe.

―――― in Hampton Roads. This, then, was the grand ren-
1862. dezvous for the Burnside Expedition.

From the decks of the steamboat could be seen the ruins of Hampton Village burned by the *Evidences* rebels, and near by, the old Fortress looking very *of War.* quiet but showing some ugly teeth in the shape of big guns, and a large number of them. Opposite the Fort is Sewall's Point and the Rip-Raps, while Norfolk is not far away. Some distance in the rear of Fortress Monroe we saw tents and barracks, which denoted large bodies of soldiers gathered here.

It was about noon of January 12th, 1862, that the fleet of Burnside sailed from Fortress Monroe, and passing between Capes Charles and Henry, soon headed south; and many were talking of the Carolina coast as the destination of the expedition. The wind blew quite fresh as we passed out of the *Coast* bay into the Atlantic, and it was interesting to see *Voyage.* how some sailing vessels went past us, and in a very short time. Keeping the coast in sight we pushed on till dark when we came to anchor, and on the morning of the 13th hastened on, with an angry sky over us and a heavy sea tossing us about, and causing many of the soldiers to pay the customary tribute to old Neptune. Still keeping in sight of land, we steamed on rounding Cape Hatteras, and in the early afternoon reached Hatteras Inlet. A small tug-boat, dancing on the waves like a cork, met us near the entrance to the Inlet; we followed close in its wake, and were soon safely anchored in the waters of Pamlico Sound, in close proximity to a rebel earthwork known as Fort Clark, which had been captured by Butler. Meantime the storm had burst upon us, and was now raging furiously; and we considered ourselves fortunate in getting in as we did. The vessels of the fleet came in rapidly like frightened sea-birds before the tempest blast, and we began to be crowded here at our anchorage ground. We saw a large ocean steamer attempt to enter the Inlet, strike on the bar outside, and sink. Tug-boats were sent to her assistance but could render none, and there she remained till next day when boats were again sent out and succeeded in bringing off the crew of the steamer, which proved to be the *City of New York*. The vessel and cargo were a total loss.

It was certainly a wild picture to look upon. In every direction the waves were running high, and tossing the vessels about in the wildest confusion; and night settled down over the scene with an increasing fury in the howling storm. Few turned

1862.

Hatteras Inlet.

Gloomy Prospect.

1862. —— in that night without gloomy forebodings for the morrow.

Great Storm.

Tuesday, January 14th, found, as was anticipated, an increasing tempest, and the vessels of the fleet all too close together for safety. This morning a steamer came crashing down upon us, running her bows into the afterpart of the *New York*, and ripping clean off one side of the after cabin in which our band slept, making it lively for them for a few minutes. Soon after, another steamer came thumping away at our bows, smashing things; and between the two the old *New York* was pretty badly used. The night before, the gunboat *Zouave*, having on board two companies of the Twenty-fifth Regiment, got to thumping on her own anchor—as report has it—jammed a hole in her bottom, and this morning sunk. The men were taken off, but boat and cargo were lost. Signals of distress were flying in all directions, and it looked bad for Burnside's fleet. Besides, it was reported that there was a bar inside which had only seven and a half feet of water on it, and our largest vessels, of which the *New York* was one, drew over eight feet. Things looked dark enough now, certainly.

Disasters.

.

January 15th the storm still continued, and we had a gunboat alongside us grinding up the fancy work on the old *New York*, but doing no great damage. To-day we noticed several soldiers were buried on the sandy shore, waves and winds making wild funeral music. Jan. 16th the colonel and surgeon of the Ninth New Jersey were drowned by the upsetting of their boat. The storm continued to rage on the 17th, and the steamer *Suwanee* got aground, and one schooner sunk. January 18th, we counted 120 vessels in the inlet, all badly crowded in this dismal, god-forsaken hole. Gen. Burnside came along to-day, looking as cheerful as if all was going well. A wonderful courage that man must have had.

1862.

Continued Disaster.

The storm at last subsided, and it was very fortunate, for our rations were running low. Hard bread, the great staple, held out, and coffee, too, though the daily allowance of each was short. Worst of all the water gave out, and a heavy rain was a godsend; for all of the rain water that could be caught was saved in barrels by the steamboat officers, and stolen—a great deal of it— by the soldiers of the Twenty-fifth. We had a nice way of filling our canteens from the water casks of the steamboat. Before leaving Worcester our too kind

Storm abates.

—— friends had provided many of the soldiers with "drinking tubes," a new thing—patented of course—possessing wonderful properties. It consisted of a small flexible rubber tube, perhaps two and a half feet long, with a mouth-piece at one end and a marvelous patent strainer or filter at the other. Place the strainer in the muddiest of ditch water, insert the mouth-piece between the lips of the thirsty soldier, and by applying the science of suction, from the most stagnant and slimy pool nothing but the purest cool spring water would be drawn into the soldier's stomach. Consequently no sickness would arise from drinking any water found on the marches. Consequently a great number of lives would be preserved, millions of money saved, the strength of the Union armies increased, and the Rebellion crushed a great deal quicker. Consequently every soldier should have one in his knapsack, and all for the trifling sum of twenty-five cents. It is difficult to estimate how much sooner the Rebellion would have been quelled if all the Union soldiers had been supplied with drinking tubes. I never saw the tubes used save on one march; some half dozen soldiers attempted to use them, but the effort was a failure; and they whirled the tubes into the bushes, with

1862.

Patent Drinking Tubes.

the remark: "Damn the things," an expression too common among the soldiers. However, the drinking tubes worked well in filling canteens from the water casks of the steamboat; by inserting one end into the bunghole of the barrel, and getting the water started we had a very good syphon, and the canteens were filled quickly, and what was better, without noise. As the water got low in the barrel, we added another length of "drinking tube"; and in this way we obtained fresh water until the discovery of the trick put an end to that little scheme.

1862.

How we obtained Water.

We had at last to resort to water distilled from salt water. This was done on the gunboats. It was warm and sickish when first obtained, though quite palatable when cold. As the storm subsided boats got along with rations, and we fared better during our stay at Hatteras.

On the 21st of January, private Tucker of Company B, died and was buried ashore. On the 28th comrade George E. Curtis of Company A died. He was sent to the Hospital Ship, and died there. This was the first death in Company A. He was twenty-one years old, of a quiet, retiring disposition, and his loss was keenly felt by his tentmates. He was buried in a little church yard about three miles from us, and his grave marked with a wooden slab.

First Death in the Company.

Life on the steamer *New York* was not, to draw it mild, of the most enjoyable sort. Eight hundred soldiers with all their traps, on one steamboat (although ours was a large one) was crowding things; and add to that the terrible stormy weather, running short of rations, water giving out, and other inconveniences, it was indeed a tedious life; and all sorts of expedients were resorted to in the endeavor to wear away the time. In the officers' quarters they got up theatricals with songs, music, etc., while the private soldiers amused themselves by writing letters home, reading, smoking, playing cards, and stealing from the sutler. Lieut. McConville came into the quarters of the men occasionally, and with Private Fairbanks of Company A, sung many songs which gave great delight to the boys and were fully appreciated by them. January 25th they began to get vessels over the bar, the lighter ones crossing without much trouble. This is a great place for wrecks. We counted thirteen between Cape Hatteras and the Inlet as we passed along, and we added to the number. The ill-fated steamer, *City of New York*, went to pieces to-day, and a large number of casks of powder came floating by us from her wreck, and were picked up by the crew of our steamer.

On the 22nd of January we steamed about a quarter of a mile further into the bay to escape the crowding of the vessels, and to prepare to cross the bar. In a dark night to look out on the fleet around us was like looking at a factory village in the evening, the large vessels appearing like cotton mills lighted up. We were lying near the *Northerner*, with the Twenty-first Massachusetts on board; and a day or two after she swung around and gave us a pretty smart raking. Our rations run short again, and a supper of hard-tack and brakish water is not, to say the least, like the supper at the Philadelphia Cooper Shop. But soldiers make merry over such things, and Old Posey said grace over our dinner of a few hard-tack: "We thank thee, Oh Quartermaster Brown, for the bountiful supply of hard-tack thou hast seen fit to bestow upon us, but for God's sake sprinkle in a little soft bread with it, or there wont be a tooth left in the Twenty-fifth Regiment."

Our Orderly was a man of varied talents. He had been a great reader in his day, and was possessed of one of those frightful memories that retain everything they once grasp. In his younger days he came under the notice of Old Doctor John Green of Worcester, who took an interest in him, and gave

1862.

Night scene.

him the run of his library. Johnson profited by this, and would talk about and quote from books of which probably nine-tenths of the regiment had never heard. He would repeat whole chapters from the Bible, and many poems. Old Posey had a great talent with his pencil, and fairly reveled in caricature; and while at Annapolis made drawings of several of the officers of the Regiment, very nicely executed, but a slight touch of his pencil converted them into broad burlesques. One day on the steamer *New York*, while at Hatteras Inlet, he got hold of a sermon by Rev. Mr. Cutler of Worcester, entitled "The Right of the Sword." He gave it a very careful reading, pronounced it "a pretty damned good thing," and went to playing the game of solitaire with his greasy old pack of cards, which kept him quiet for hours. Old Posey was a mixture of queer materials, rough outside, but a kind heart within. He was greatly addicted to smoking, card playing, Bible reading, and profanity. We shall see him at Cold Harbor.

On the 26th of January we went on board the small steamer *Pilot Boy*, and were taken to the ferry boat *Eagle*, where we spent a few days of wretchedness, with little to eat, and crowded almost beyond

endurance. We could only anxiously wait for the ——
New York to be worked over the bar that we might 1862.
return to our old quarters. An *incident* occurred
on the *Eagle* at this time—*incidents* are always oc-
curring in a soldier's life—that was quite amusing.

Our sutler (H. O. Clark) had left a barrel of sugar *A stray*
on board the *New York*, and strange to say, there *Barrel of Sugar.*
seemed to be no one to look after it. Consequently
it was removed with the soldiers and their traps to
the *Eagle*—a very bad place to put a barrel of sugar.
It was discovered at once by the boys, the barrel
head was knocked in, tin cups appeared as by magic,
and in a "short space of period" as the boys would
say, an empty sugar barrel was tossed into the sea ;
and every haversack on the boat was puffed out with
its sweet contents. Soldiers always know how to
take advantage of circumstances—this was a circumstance. This barrel of sugar was quite a find for us.
We used to *find* a great many things just this way.
Stealing ? Oh no ; it was considered perfectly square
to *find* things from the sutler. He got it all back,
and more too, in his charges for what *honest* soldiers
bought of him. It was a common case of "Now you
see it, and now you don't,"—this sugar business—a
law, by the way, that always worked well in the

army. Solids or liquids, it made no difference—all went well. This find of sugar lasted us a few days. It is a fact, however, that with all our watchfulness and care, we never found another barrel of sugar.

Saturday, February 1st, the *New York* was, after a deal of trouble, dragged across the bar, and we returned to our old quarters on board. The bunks in the center of the cabin had been taken down in our absence, and the men were now obliged to sleep on the floor.

Return to the New York

On the 3d of February the scene changed entirely from a disheartening, to a decidedly encouraging one. The wind had gone down, and the seas were calm, vessels all across the bar, decks crowded with soldiers, and everything ready for business. The morning of February 5th broke calm and pleasant; the sun, rising clear and beautiful, shed a radiant light over the fleet of Burnside, the dreary sands of Hatteras, and the stormy seas on which we had tossed so long. Far out at sea a solitary sail, a mere speck in the distance, was working its way northward, while nearer, but outside the Inlet, the big waves were rolling in and breaking on the sandy shore, leaving long lines and patches of white foam. Meanwhile all was excitement in the Inlet.

At 8 o'clock, A. M., the fleet was getting under way with bands playing and flags flying. The gunboats took the lead, followed first by the *New Brunswick* with the Tenth Connecticut on board, and second by the *New York* with the Twenty-fifth Massachusetts, having three schooners in tow. The fleet consisted of some thirty gunboats, nine or ten steamers with troops on board, and numerous sailing vessels, perhaps sixty to seventy-five all told. Each vessel had its counterpart or image in the water below, and the whole scene, bathed in the rosy light of morning, formed a singularly beautiful picture, never before witnessed by any of those present, and unlikely to be again during a lifetime. It was in striking contrast to the days of wretchedness we had so lately passed in this same spot. Thus, after a tedious delay of twenty-three days, the Burnside Expedition was once more on the move and about to take the aggressive.

The fleet sailed slowly along, and certainly a more magnificent sight was never before seen on this side of the Atlantic. The waves as though tired out with the struggle of the past three weeks, had quieted down, and we were gliding along as peacefully over the waters of this inland sea as if its surface had

1862.

The Fleet moves.

1862. —— never been disturbed by other than the gentlest of breezes. Thus the hours passed till about two in the afternoon, when the fleet came to anchor half way to Roanoke Island, the transports together, with the gunboats outside as protection for the fleet. We had orders to land in light marching order, that is, without knapsacks; and at night the lights were put out or concealed. The night was beautiful, clear and quiet; and from the other steamers we heard the low strains of music, and voices singing—

"On the other side of Jordan,"

and

"There is rest for the weary."

"It may be the last night's rest for some of us,—no doubt we may be on the other side of Jordan; but what is the use? We will pass this night in quiet if possible, and let what follows take care of itself." This was a soldier's reasoning.

About 8 A. M. of February 6th the fleet started again in the same order as before, the gunboats taking the lead. It clouded up just after sunrise, and rained quite steadily till noon, when we anchored *Roanoke Island.* again with Roanoke Island in sight ahead. In the afternoon a tugboat came alongside and reported that the gunboat *Ranger* was ordered into action, and that we must make room for fifty men of the Twenty-seventh Regiment who were on board. Our gunboats had discovered the Rebel fleet, so that there was to be work upon the water as well as on the land. Soon after the *Ranger* came alongside and left two hundred men instead of fifty, all belonging to the Twenty-seventh. This made over nine hundred men on our good old steamer. We remained here all night.

1862.

February 7th opened with a fog, but it cleared away about nine. Gen. Foster came up in the little steamer *Picket*, and addressing Col. Upton, said: "Be ready to start at any moment. We shall move up to the Island and give you all a chance to witness the bombardment. Then we shall land and clean out those fellows at once." This was received with the wildest cheering, and soon after we moved on towards Roanoke Island.

Gen. Foster's order.

CHAPTER V.

THE BATTLE OF ROANOKE.

1862.

Defenses of the Island.

THE DEFENSES of the Island, it was reported, consisted of Fort Huger, Fort Blanchard and Fort Bartow, all on the western shore of Roanoke. The first, with twelve guns, was near the northern end of the Island; and next in order Fort Blanchard with three guns. Still farther to the south, and perhaps nearly midway of the Island, was Fort Bartow with ten guns. From near this point to the main land of North Carolina a line of piles or sunken ships extended, and behind or north of these defenses was the rebel fleet consisting of eight small vessels with ten or twelve guns all told. The water between Roanoke Island and the main land is known as Croatan Sound. About midway, and running lengthwise of the Island, was the regular road; and near the center of the Island was a three-gun battery which was flanked on either side by swamps supposed to be impassable. The guns of this battery perfectly commanded the road, which was the only way, apparently, to the northern end of the Island, where were the camps of the Rebels. Here, then, was the work to be done: the fleet to silence the forts and destroy the Rebel vessels; the army to land and clean out the Island.*

1862.

The transports came to anchor just off the place known as Ashby's Landing, and we had a splendid chance to witness the whole affair. We watched with eager interest our gunboats as they took their positions apparently in easy range of the Rebel forts, and not a gun fired, when suddenly there was a puff of smoke from one of our gunboats, a report showing a heavy gun had been fired, and the bombardment of Roanoke Island was begun. This was about half-past eleven on the morning of February 7th. The first shot struck the Rebel earthwork squarely, and an explosion quickly followed throwing up smoke and dirt, showing that the shot had done its work. The fort promptly replied, and as

Attack begun.

---

* Roanoke Island, from this distance, had the appearance for the most part of being well wooded, with but one house in sight, or rather one house with a small out-building in the rear. These were near what was called Ashby's Landing, which was the point where we expected to land.

1862. —— the gunboats, one after another, came into action, we had passing before our eyes a scene such as we all had undoubtedly read of, but probably what few of us had ever witnessed—a bombardment.

The bombardment. The movements of a little sloop were watched by all with great interest. It had one gun only, said to be a hundred pounder. It sailed in a circle and put a shot into the Rebel fort every time on its nearest approach to it. It was an exciting scene; the gunboats firing so slowly and yet so surely, every shot seeming to tell on the fort, while the enemy's fire, much more rapid, appeared to have no effect whatever on the fleet. May be the range was too great, or perhaps bad gunnery was the reason ; but, so far as we could see, little damage was done to the Union gunboats. Thus the battle went on. We moved up nearer to the scene of conflict and had a still better view of the engagement. The gunboats were now firing much more rapidly than at the commencement, and the fort was apparently about silenced, when suddenly great clouds of smoke rolled up from it, showing that the interior was on fire. At this cheers went up from every vessel of the Union fleet, and the gunboats kept firing with the greatest rapidity.

The Rebel fleet meantime we had heard nothing of; a weak demonstration attempted towards the last of the bombardment was quickly repulsed by a few shots from the Union gunboats.

About 3 P. M. we were ordered to land, and the Twenty-fifth Regiment went from the *New York* on board the *Pilot Boy*, and towing a long line of boats filled with men, moved slowly towards the land. We had seen the glitter of Rebel bayonets as we left the *New York*, and all expected a volley as we approached the land, but a few shells from our gunboat, *Delaware*, sent the Rebels "kiting," and we received not a single shot from them while landing. When the *Pilot Boy* approached the land as near as was possible, the boys were transferred to boats alongside, which were quickly filled. The desire to go in the first boats was so great, it was only by repeated orders from Capt. Pickett himself that those who were to stay behind could be kept quiet; and all were promised, "you shall go in the next boats." Capt. Pickett, Orderly George A. Johnson and the right of the Company were in the first boats. At the same time the long line of boats astern separated, and all made for the shore. It was an exciting time, and we watched anxiously to see who

Orders to land.

would reach land first. The boats containing the Company A boys had the advantage and touched ground first, but it was the muddy bottom, not dry land; but no sooner had the boats struck ground than the men were in the water wading for the shore. Capt. Pickett was the first man in the water. We could see from the *Pilot Boy* the men holding up their rifles and cartridge boxes to keep them from getting wet. Capt. Pickett and George A. Johnson, our Orderly Sergeant, were the first to stand on dry land;* and we who were left behind on the old *Pilot Boy* made the air ring with cheers for the pony Captain of Company A. Thus, February 7th, 1862, we scored one for the old Company, as Captain Josiah Pickett and Orderly Sergeant George A. Johnson were the first men of the Burnside Expedition to stand on Roanoke Island.

The boats returning (the distance was but a few rods), a sort of bridge was made of them, and the

---

* It has been claimed that Lieut. Andrew of the Ninth New York, in reconnoitring for a landing place for the troops, took soundings to the shore of Roanoke, and actually stood on the Island. Of the correctness of this report I cannot judge. It is also said that the Lieut. was fired on and several of his boat's crew (5th R. I.) wounded. All of this may be true so far as I know; but I simply claim what we all saw—that at the *landing* of troops on the 7th of February, Capt. Pickett and Orderly Sergeant Johnson of Co. A, Twenty-fifth Mass. were *first* to land on the Island.

soldiers got ashore much faster and with dry clothes. The Company was quickly formed and deployed as skirmishers. The house we had seen from the steamer was surrounded and the door burst open. The occupants had fled, but a fire was blazing upon the hearth, the table stood loaded with dishes, and everything denoted a hasty departure. Behind the house was a smaller one, evidently the servants' quarters. This was much in the same condition as the first, not a human being to be found. In a small out-building we found fresh bread and a pan of milk; this was a prize, and in a few minutes both bread and milk had vanished, and we left the place thinking how nicely everything works in for a soldier.

It was now growing dark, and we prepared to bivouac. It began to rain later, but our fires burnt cheerily, and the boys brought along rails to replenish them, and all sorts of things to eat. How nicely rails work in for fires—just the right size and so dry! And then the fact is, soldiers are always hungry, and it is part of a soldier's duty to bring in to his squad round the bivouac fire something in the way of rations, and nothing comes amiss that can be eaten or drank, or in any way used for the comfort of the squad. One brought a chunk of salt pork—

1862.

Soldiers bivouac.

good; another, onions—good again; another cabbages; another, an old iron kettle. Corporal Jaalam Gates brought a back-load of sweet potatoes. It seems the Corporal had found a lot of potatoes, and no way to "tote" them along. He quickly took off his drawers, tied up the legs, filled them with the coveted potatoes, and brought them on his back to our bivouac amid the shouts of the boys as he made his appearance. So with roasting potatoes in the ashes, boiling them with pork and cabbage in our kettle, and making our coffee in our tin cups over the rail fire, we managed to get up quite a supper; and we were feeling very comfortable in spite of the rain, when, about nine P. M., we were startled by the hoarse cry of the Orderly, "Fall in, Company A; fall in." We are quickly in line, and file off directly into the forest which surrounds the little clearing where we landed. We steal along rapidly and silently, not a word spoken; and leave a guard of two or three men at every path that crosses the road. We come to a small stream and have to pass through it; it is waist deep and we are thoroughly soaked, but on we go. A light is seen a short distance from the road, and Sergeant J. J. McLane is sent to look after it; he approaches it cautiously

1862.

Timely supplies.

Midnight Reconnaissance.

and reports on his return that it is evidently a bivouac fire of the enemy. We are soon after ordered back, and pass through the stream of water again, and after a short halt once more ordered forward through the water for the third time. Sergeant George Burr is left at one cross road with three men, and thus we move on till at last we have orders to return to our bivouac which we reach about midnight, having crossed that wretched stream of water four times; and return to our starting point wet, cold and tired.

Stirring up our fire we cooked some coffee which revived us somewhat, and in the driving rain we curled up on the wet ground and passed a wretched night in the vain endeavor to sleep, and eagerly wishing for the morrow.

"I was quite fortunate in having a dry pair of stockings to put on after we got back from our scouting expedition. Taking off the soaked brogans and wet socks, I proceeded to put on a clean dry pair, when—'Where in thunder did you get dry stockings?' 'Ain't you slatting on considerable style for a soldier?' 'Look here, fellows, Sergeant's got clean, dry stockings,' and other exclamations. 'You ain't putting on any airs; oh no,' said a dis-

1862.

Dry Stockings.

consolate looking soldier who had been casting longing eyes during the transfer. 'Home made, hey, boy?' 'Well, boys, these *are* home made. My old mother knit them—God bless her—and I've carried them right up here in the lining of my vest, one on each side, heels front and toes to the shoulder, don't you see. Now if you fellows want to know just how uncomfortable you are, feel of that warm, dry stocking;' and from hand to hand went the stocking, stroked like a cat by one, rubbed on the cheek of another, with all sorts of comments on the mysterious appearance of dry stockings in such wet weather. So after washing as well as I could the socks just taken off, and sticking them up by the fire to dry if possible, I found them dry enough in the morning to take their place in the vest as the others had done. This plan of carrying an extra pair of stockings worked well, and many made use of it when a long march was anticipated."

February 8th we were early astir, and hard-tack, sweet potatoes baked in the ashes, and a cup (holding a quart) of coffee, made a breakfast fit for a soldier. About seven we again heard the hoarse voice of our Orderly ("Old Posey"), with "Fall in, Company A"; again we were quickly in line, and again we marched directly into the forest in the same road we took the night before. Again we crossed that miserable stream of water and again were soaked through to our waists. But we were soon deployed as skirmishers on both sides of the road, and we advanced slowly on account of the dense tangled undergrowth, the country being one great swamp. This was no picnic, no fancy skirmish we were on; it meant business this time. After perhaps an hour of this work—it seemed much longer than that—we heard the sharp crack of a rifle on our left, and immediately the cry ran along the line, "Here they are—here they are." We had run on to the Rebel pickets, and with a cheer we struggled through the almost impassable swamp. Capt. Pickett, who had all this time been encouraging us, now shouted his orders, and his voice rang out loud and clear like a bugle-tone. "Give it to 'em, lads; drive 'em out! Drive the devils out of that!" We responded with a cheer, but it was terrible work. How the sweat rolled off our faces. How the brambles and briars clung to us, tearing our clothes, and flesh even. It was exciting though, for all that. We were exchanging shots with the enemy every rod, and were driving them right along.

1862. Feb. 8. Battle of Roanoke.

Struggle in the Swamp.

—— We came at last to a large clearing extending on both sides of the road; the trees had been felled and lay on the ground, and our unpractised eyes told us that we had driven the Rebel pickets to their stronghold. On closer inspection we could see the outline of an earthwork mounting three guns in embrasures, at perhaps two hundred yards distance. Here, then, was the work to be done. The guns in the earthwork commanded the road and the open space. But we had got to clean out those fellows —that's what Gen. Foster said we should do. We came to a halt, and as skirmishers took advantage of the situation all we could. Every hollow in the ground had a soldier in it; every tree had a soldier behind it. We covered ourselves as best we could, which as skirmishers we had a right to do; and obeying the order of our Captain, "Don't waste your powder, boys," we fired carefully, and took great pains that we fired at something, and we never aimed at trees. We fired lying down, and rolled over on our backs to load. In skirmishing, the men are kept five yards apart; we had followed this rule to a nicety, so that Company A, nearly one hundred men, stretched out a long distance at

1862. Feb. 8. Battle of Roanoke.

Skirmishing.

this time, and the firing was of course very irregular, each shooting as he found a proper mark.

The enemy fired much as we did, slowly; and had got our range to a dot. Suddenly we noticed one of the Company crawling to the rear dragging his rifle along with him. "Hallo, Dave, what's the trouble?" "Hit, fellers," was his short reply, and he crawled along a short distance, and then cooly got up and walked limping to the rear. This was David B. Bigelow, the first man of Company A wounded in action in the service of the United States. He was hit in the left leg, in the fleshy part above the knee—a bloody and painful, but not a serious wound.

1862.
Feb. 8.
Battle of Roanoke.
First man wounded.

The bullets came uncomfortably near, and so spiteful. "Those fellows mean to hit us, Captain," said Dan Eaton. "Don't you mean to hit them?" said the Captain. "Of course I do, but you see—" He did not finish the sentence but pulled out a plug of tobacco and bit off a generous allowance, and running his cold gray eye along his rifle barrel, we heard in a few seconds its sharp, spiteful ring, which showed that he meant to hit *something*—not a tree.

Another man went to the rear—Horace Brooks, hit in the foot, and he limped away out of sight.

<small>1862.
Feb. 8.
Battle of Roanoke.</small>　It is singular that a wounded man will walk away from the spot where he receives his wound as though he could not be hit again. This wound of Brooks crippled him for life. He never served with the Company again, but remained his three years as a detailed man at New Berne.

We expected the Regiment would soon make its appearance with the Brigade, when we would be withdrawn as skirmishers, and take our places with them in line of battle. It should be remembered that this was our first experience under fire, and it must be confessed that the boys showed a deal of pluck and endurance in skirmishing up to this point, <small>*Coolness under fire*</small> and great coolness in action. This, undoubtedly, was in a great measure owing to the thorough drill we had received from the first; also to the cool behavior of the officers. The orders of Capt. Pickett were clearly and promptly given, and we felt from one end of the skirmish line to the other that he was with us, and that he was in command. Lieut. Goodwin showed great ability and coolness through the whole affair, and these officers could not feel otherwise than pleased with the behavior of the men in this their first trial. Lieut. Bessey had been detailed on the signal corps and was not with the Company in the Battle of Roanoke.

1862. Feb. 8.

As we expected, the Regiment soon made its appearance with the rest of the Brigade, and we took our place in its ranks; but Samuel S. Dresser went down with a wound in his leg, Charley Bartlett with a hit in the arm, and Henry F. Knox with a wound in the neck—five of Company A wounded in the first engagement.

Battle of Roanoke.

Line of battle was formed as soon as possible, and the Rebels opened on us with the big guns. We replied with a volley of musketry, and the battle was fairly opened. Our artillery (small howitzers) was soon placed in position, and for some three hours the firing was incessant. The ammunition of the Twenty-fifth being exhausted, the Regiment was withdrawn to the rear a short distance, and we rested on the ground. While in this position Hawkin's Zouaves (9th N. Y. Vols.) came up the road at double-quick, and we supposed were going to charge the enemy at once; but they halted near and in front of us, and by some mistake or other, fired a volley into the Tenth Connecticut. Some said they were deceived by the gray over-

Mistake of the Zouaves

coats of the Connecticut troops, that being the color worn by the Rebels. Be it as it may, the Tenth turned on the Zouaves to see from whence the firing came, and the latter faced about and made tracks for the rear, nearly running over us (the 25th). This was prevented by the boys springing to their feet and bringing their rifles to "Charge bayonets," the officers cooly drawing their swords and giving the orders. This stopped the backward movement and prevented much trouble.

*1862.
Feb. 8.
Battle of Roanoke.*

A Panic averted.

We had an opportunity while lying here of seeing the effect of the enemy's firing, in the bringing out of the wounded. One man was carried by with his head nearly all torn away by a cannon shot; another had an arm shot off, but he walked by cheering on the soldiers as they fired. Another, shot in the breast, was moaning terribly and leaning on the shoulders of two of his comrades. Many were brought out on stretchers, and many dead were carried hurriedly by. Thus the grim and ghastly procession passed on.

Dead and wounded.

Meantime the Twenty-first Massachusetts and Fifty-first New York had pushed deep into the swamp on the left, with the intention of flanking the Rebel right ; the Twenty-third Massachusetts and Ninth New York (Hawkins Zouaves) tried the same on the Rebel left. After a hard struggle with the mud and briars of this miserable swamp, the brave regiments on the left succeeded in flanking the Rebel right, and with a sudden dash and rousing cheers, entered the Rebel battery. The colors of the Twenty-first Massachusetts were the first to float over the Rebel works, quickly followed by those of the Fifty-first New York. History has it (notably Abbott's History of the Rebellion) that Hawkins' Zouaves stormed the battery and took it. This is simply untrue. The Hawkins Zouaves, with the Twenty-third Massachusetts "swarmed over the earthworks," possibly; but the battery was *taken* already. The Zouaves no doubt had a good writer among them, and he wrote a very creditable story; but what is the use? The Twenty-first Massachusetts, that splendid fighting regiment, *first* entered and its colors first floated over the Rebel battery.

*1862.
Feb. 8.
Battle of Roanoke.*

Battery taken.

We had orders now to move on, and we advanced quickly up the road and were soon inside the battery. We counted fifteen dead Rebels lying around in the earthworks, most of them. The first was a gunner, struck in the head by a bullet. His cap was on his head, strap under his chin, just gasping

*1862.
Feb. 8.
Battle of Roanoke.*

—— his last as we passed. The ground was covered with his blood. All of the Rebels killed were poorly clad with one exception. That was a young man, a captain, said to be Captain Cole and to belong to Philadelphia. He wore a fine uniform, had rings on his fingers and gold studs in his white shirt front. He was killed by a shot through the heart. The bullet made a small, clean round hole, which had bled scarcely a drop.

Rebel dead.

We continued our march through the woods, passing very few houses, and taking a few prisoners who seemed willing enough to be captured. These also were poorly clad, but were quite talkative. We soon met one of Burnside's aids, who said the Rebels had surrendered over two thousand men, and more than twenty pieces of artillery. So ended the Battle of Roanoke Island, after a struggle of three hours or more, and a total loss to the Union troops of forty killed and over two hundred wounded.

As we pushed along rapidly we found the road thickly strewn with guns and equipments, knapsacks and clothing, thrown hastily away by the Rebels in their flight. We passed one house near the road filled with wounded Rebels, among them

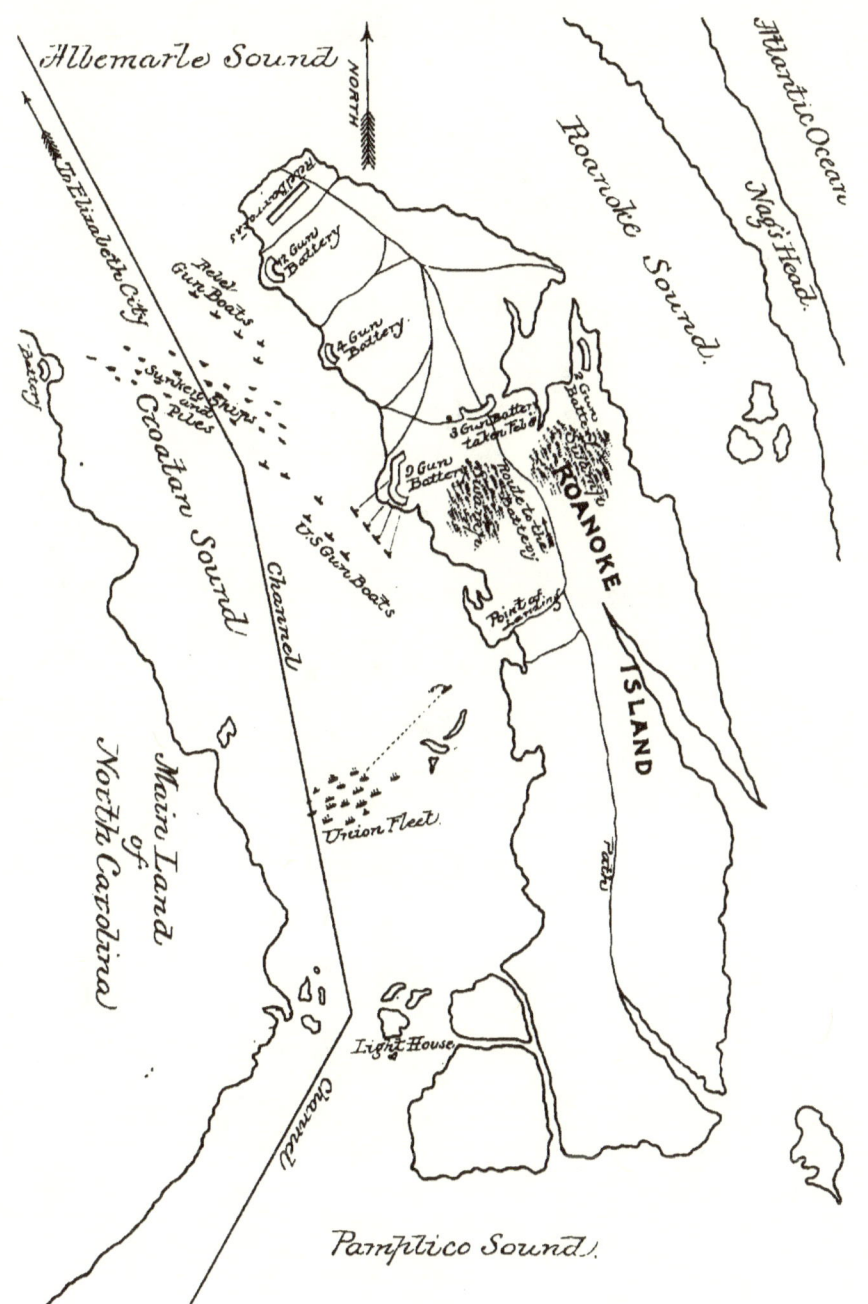

O. Jennings Wise, son of Henry A. Wise, of Virginia. He was badly wounded and died soon after.

1862.

Our road·lay through woods the greater part of the way. We passed on our right several small hills which appeared to be composed entirely of clean sand, with no vegetation on them save an occasional stunted pine; but nothing green whatever, and presenting a curious sight. It was dark when we reached the Rebel encampment, and we were quite ready to halt when the order was given. We found here very extensive barracks, and an immense amount of army material in the shape of rations, ammunition, guns, swords and other small arms. The barracks were very well built of logs, and could shelter eight or ten thousand men. We found room in the building after considerable search, and we were glad to get under cover.

Rebel encampment.

It was interesting to see how freely our boys and the Rebels talked over the events of the day together. Many of the Rebels did not seem to care much about getting beaten, and many said they were forced into the service.

The next day (Feb. 9th) was the Sabbath. It did not seem much like a Sunday at home, and there was so much stir and excitement that it was a great contrast to our quiet Sundays at Annapolis. Our camp here was known as Camp Foster. The Rebels were everywhere about, apparently under no restraint whatever. They were all as poorly clothed as the first we had seen, save the officers who in general were very well clad; but in no case did they compare with the boys in blue.

1862.

In the afternoon a few of us got passes and started on an expedition to the northern shore of the Island, extending our tramp to the two upper forts captured the day before. The first one and the largest, Fort Huger, mounted twelve guns, mostly thirty-two pounders. The other, Fort Blanchard, was a much smaller earthwork, containing but three guns. These forts were but just finished, and were not used in the battle of the 8th. The guns had been spiked, but only with nails which could be easily removed. The small fort was about two miles from the larger, and both were regular earthworks and really quite strong. We found the road we travelled thickly strewn with knapsacks and other accoutrements.

Tramp over the Island.

Returning to camp we found our squad had a good dinner nearly prepared. Good dinners are obstacles easily overcome by hungry soldiers. Sergeant "Jemsy" (McLane) had been skirmishing around for something to eat—soldiers always do when off duty—and had brought in a nice fat turkey; another had confiscated a chicken, both boiled together with a good bit of pork and plenty of sweet potatoes. Who wouldn't go for a soger?*

1862.

Just after dinner we were startled by a volley of musketry and bullets flying over our heads. "Fall in, fall in," was the order; and in a very few minutes we were in line and ready for action. Eating dinner a few minutes ago; now ready to be shot! The Rebel prisoners bustled around considerable, their officers appearing at the doors of the barracks, looking anxiously around, expecting as we were that trouble was brewing; but the firing proved to be by some of the Union troops, who had discharged their rifles preparatory to a good cleaning, and had aimed a little too close to our heads to be agreeable. But we had no more of this, so we broke ranks and the camp settled down into quietude again.

Alarm.

The results of the victory of February 8th may be briefly stated. Two thousand five hundred prisoners, three forts containing twenty-five guns, one small earthwork where the fight took place having three guns, and another not used in the action also

Fruits of Victory.

* A common expression in the army.

—— having three guns, small arms by thousands, tons of ammunition, and a great quantity of flour, bacon, etc., while the Rebel fleet was wholly destroyed. Truly, a first-class victory.

1862.

Burdened as we were with so many prisoners, it required a regiment daily for guard duty; but this did not last many days, for on February 11th the Rebel officers were sent away to be exchanged. They marched from the barracks to the place of embarkation between two lines of Union soldiers, and went on board the *S. R. Spaulding*. This was some relief; and other prisoners went off later, lightening up the guard and making an easier life of it.

Rebel Officers depart.

The prisoners and Union boys would often get together evenings, and talk of the events of the last few days in perfect good feeling; and sometimes the Rebel prisoners held prayer meetings in which our boys would join. Singular circumstance,— killing one another a few hours before, now praying that each others' lives might be spared. Our boys swapped jack knives with the Rebels, and traded all sorts of things for tobacco; and when we saw the boys in blue and the boys in gray exchanging the very buttons on their jackets (those who had them)

Friendly Intercourse.

and pleased as children, it did seem as if the habit of swapping could hardly be carried further.

The prisoners were for the most part extremely ignorant, and many expressed a wish to get back home and to stay there. The officers seemed to think they had made a great mistake in allowing us to land as they did without hindrance. No doubt about that. Ten thousand armed men—real live Yankees—once on Roanoke Island, were going to travel from one end to the other, and no earthly power could stop them. It was a mistake; but the landing would have been made and the Rebels cleaned out anyway—didn't Gen. Foster say so?

We learned from the darky servants of the Rebel officers that their masters had buried "lots of things out in de woods dar." That was enough; our boys gave the woods "out dar" a thorough search, digging up the ground with their bayonets and knives, and finding many small arms, some very nice revolvers, several fancy rifles, and many other things of no great value. One squad did not get very well paid for their trouble, for they found after some patient digging that they had opened the grave of a dead Rebel. There was not so much digging after that.

Digging for Treasure.

Among the prisoners taken were men from the Wise Legion of Virginia, Richmond Blues, Ben McCulloch Rangers, and the Eighth North Carolina Regiment. These were considered among the best troops, and best clothed and equipped.

On the morning of February 16th a lot of prisoners under guard of Company A, were marched to the shore near the upper fort, where each prisoner took his backload of boards and brought them to the barracks. This was not fancied much by the Rebels, although there was not a great deal of growling; but I think the movement rather pleased Company A. The boards were to be used in building, so the movement was to some purpose.

A squad of us tried the experiment of taking a swim at a sandy beach we found at the northern end of the Island, but the coldness of the water drove us out as quickly as we went in, and the swim ended in a very short bath; and we made up our minds that bathing at Roanoke Island in February was not as agreeable as bathing in Massachusetts in July. The changes in the weather we found about as sudden and as great as those in New England.

On the 17th a large number of prisoners left under guard of the Twenty-third Massachusetts; and on the 18th all that remained of the prisoners were marched under guard of the Twenty-fifth Regiment to the shore near Fort Huger, where they were put on board the *Pilot Boy* and the "Old Wheelbarrow,"* as the stern-wheel steamer was called. On going on board the vessels the prisoners had to march directly under the old flag that they had so dishonored a few days before by firing upon it. I think the sight did us all good, and it certainly did the prisoners no harm, for they saw floating above them the starry flag that had protected them in former years, and which was to protect them in years to come. These prisoners were like all the rest, a tough-looking set, ragged and dirty, and very illiterate. Some of our Company had found a muster roll of one of the Rebel companies, and fully two-thirds of the names had their X mark. Some said they were fighting for their

1862.

Removal of the prisoners.

Their ignorance

---

* The stern-wheel steamer or "Wheelbarrow" was a rusty old thing, much like the steamers on the western rivers. It was two stories high with a large wheel astern. It was painted black, and looked like an old tumble-down cotton mill afloat. Of very light draft, it was of great service in the shallow water, and was constantly on the go. It is a wonder how she ever got around Cape Hatteras if she was brought that way.

homes; others that they were fighting for secession; others frankly owned that they did not know what they were fighting for. Some had considerable pluck, and said they would be at us again when exchanged; and some of these same men were taken again at New Berne. Others had got enough of it and longed for home. These prisoners, most of them, were taken to the steamer *New York*, and Company A went on board as guard. We moved about two miles from the Island, near a light house, and came to anchor to wait for the other boats with the rest of the prisoners. It was said that we should sail for Elizabeth City where the prisoners would be exchanged.

1862.

Removal of the prisoners.

We lay here all day of the 19th, and not until about 2 P. M. on the 20th did we receive orders to follow the *S. R. Spaulding*, which with the other steamers had just arrived. The vessels carrying the prisoners were the *S. R. Spaulding*, *New York*, *Cossack*, *Admiral* and *Peabody*. To Elizabeth City where we were going was some forty miles, and on starting, the other steamers were all in advance of the *New York*; but we passed them one after another, the *Spaulding* included, and then to obey orders took our place second in line. It was a pretty sight to see the *New York* pass the other steamers so nicely, and the prisoners as well as our boys were greatly excited over it, and called it a race, but it was simply obeying orders.

About twenty miles from Roanoke we passed another light house, and soon began to see signs of life. Villages, wind mills, cultivated fields, etc., appeared; and the land in many places seemed to be covered with trees, pines mostly, with the dark green cypress on the low lands. About 6 P. M. we anchored off Elizabeth City, a high-sounding name for so small a village (ten or twelve hundred inhabitants), but quite a pretty place for all that. We here saw what our gunboats had been doing since the fight. It seems they drove the Rebel boats from Roanoke, and followed them to this place where they found six Rebel gunboats under the protection of a battery on shore. The Union fleet, as the story goes, paid no attention to the battery, but went heavily for the boats, boarding and capturing two and sinking four (the wrecks of which we saw sticking out of the water), clearing out the whole lot; and then paid their regards to the battery, which was quickly silenced. The troops and inhabitants fled; but the place being of no importance

Rebel fleet destroyed.

1862.

—— in a military way, it was not occupied by our men, and the inhabitants returned.

1862.

At 11 o'clock of February 21st, we steamed up to the little wharf, and began to "discharge cargo"— that is, to land the prisoners. They were gathered into companies by their sergeants, and were put ashore as fast as possible. It was a motley crowd —so wretchedly clad. Their blankets were made of bits of carpet that had evidently had hard usage before serving this purpose. There was no uniformity in their dress—it could not be called a uniform, save in color, nearly all being the same dirty gray. They had no arms of course; these were all left at Roanoke. Knapsacks and haversacks were entirely home made, with canteens made of wood. A more wretched-looking set of men I certainly never saw. Some said to us in a quiet way that they would never be caught in the army again; others were stupidly indifferent; others were somewhat excited, and a few had some bluster left; but it was a sorry sight. And yet, these men fought well in the battle of the 8th. Some of these poor fellows were sick on the boat, and we got medicine for them, took good care of them, and made them as

Prisoners landed and paroled.

comfortable as we could—indeed they were treated like men.

On shore we noticed some Rebel soldiers with our blue uniforms on. These they got from the gunboat *Fanny*, which was taken by the Rebels, and which our fleet recaptured and sunk a few days before. We were not allowed to stray from the *New York*, but we could see several church spires, and that the streets were wide, with many trees scattered along through them. We could also see the ruins of several houses burned by their own soldiers, who would have destroyed the whole town if the inhabitants had not rallied in time to save their property, so they told us. We stopped only long enough to land the prisoners, and then moved about half a mile from the town and dropped anchor to give the other steamers a chance to land their prisoners. It is an unimportant fact to note here; but how the frogs did peep that night! It seemed as if they kept up the chorus till morning. Said one of our boys: "You bet the little cusses ain't piping like that up home about this time."

February 22nd, at 8 A. M. we got under way, and after a very pleasant sail anchored off Roanoke Island once more, and listened to a salute in honor

margin: 1862. *Elizabeth City.* *Frogs.*

1862. —— of Washington's birth-day from the guns spiked by the Rebels on the day of the fight.

Sunday the 23d a boat went ashore and our knapsacks were sent to us—a soldier feels lost without his knapsack—and we soon after moved up to the first light house we saw when going to Elizabeth City; and after a stay of twenty-four hours, were ordered back to join the fleet at Roanoke.

In one of the state rooms occupied by the Rebel prisoners, we found the following lines written in pencil on the wall:

Gratitude of the prisoners. We, the non-commissioned officers of Co. K, North Carolina 8th Regiment, do give our thanks to Co. A, of the Massachusetts 25th, for the many acts of kindness shown by that Co. to us, and if it is ever in our power will return the same.

Sergt. J. IDE, for the Company

Many months after, it *was* in their power, and they redeemed their promise.

February 26th, we went ashore in small boats, landing near the spot we first touched February 8th; and from there marched to the barracks we left one week ago. We noticed lots of robins on the way up, singing as sweetly as they ever did at home in warmer weather.

Our mail had just arrived. Mail day was a great day for soldiers. The postmaster, a soldier detailed for that purpose, brought the mail to the Company, and called out the names of the lucky ones, handing over the precious letters. The Twenty-fifth is notably a writing regiment. The mail bag always leaves well filled and returns in like condition.

1862.

Mail day.

It seems almost laughable to tell now of the rumors of peace that were afloat in camp at this early stage of the war. We were all to be home in sixty days, etc. But all through the war these rumors would start up, no one knew how; but would die out as quickly as they had risen. The particular rumor at this time was that Burnside had said that he would have his troops home by the first of July. Some tried to believe it, but the majority did not take stock in this or any other report of like import.

Rumors of peace.

Our camp here was known as Camp Foster (our second camp since we left Worcester); and by order of Gen. Burnside we are to have inscribed on our banner: "Roanoke Island, February 8th, 1862." Burnside gave his troops great praise for their conduct in this their first engagement; and they certainly did well, and really deserved the commendation he bestowed on them.

Camp Foster.

1862.

While here our minds naturally went back to the discovery and first settlement of Roanoke Island in the days of Elizabeth of England, nearly three centuries before. Sir Walter Raleigh visited the Island and attempted the foundation of a colony which proved a failure. After so long a time its romantic history was now supplemented by the remarkable events of the last few days.

A tramp.

"One morning I obtained a pass, and started about 9 o'clock for a long stroll, intending to hunt up the wounded of Company A. Making my way at once to Fort Huger, and following along the coast of the Island to Fort Blanchard, I noticed a boat-load of Zouaves bound in the same direction as myself; and presently a hail came: 'Hallo, there; what regiment?' 'Twenty-fifth Massachusetts,' I replied. This answer brought the boat to me with the welcome, 'Come aboard'; and we were soon at their quarters, which proved to be on one of the old canal boats we had towed around Cape Hatteras. It was Company K, Hawkins Zouaves, into whose hands I had fallen, and a bright, jolly set of fellows they were. In vain I pleaded a long tramp before me; I must stop to dinner, and I did. These men were all quite young, and were completely bound up in

Hawkins Zouaves.

their regiment. Its singular dress they claimed was the most comfortable, for a soldier—the red cap, loose jacket and baggy trousers. Their orderly was of Scotch descent, named Donaldson, and he was quite enthusiastic over Massachusetts soldiers. He said the Zouave uniform seemed whimsical, and it was so regarded; but men will do a great deal for a whim. These men with their showy uniforms appeared well pleased with their officers, and seemed very intelligent and contented.

1862.

"I left the Zou-zous with regret, and hurried on to the house we surrounded when we first landed. This was used now as a hospital, and on going up stairs I found only one of Company A—Charley Bartlett. He was feeling badly; his right arm—the wounded one—was bandaged, and he was suffering a great deal from it. I cheered him up, told him all the news, and he said if he could only have his knapsack and be with the other wounded A boys he would be all right. I promised him this, and bade him goodbye.

Charley Bartlett.

"I learned that most of the wounded had been placed on steamers and nearly all would be sent home. I found no more A boys. Near the house were many graves of the Union dead, each having

—— a board at the head. Some were marked with name, regiment, etc.; others "supposed to be" such a one; and several were marked "unknown." This, then, was the end—an unknown grave. This is the dark side of a soldier's life—wounds, suffering, death and a nameless grave.

1862.

The dead.

"From the hospital my next point was the battery where the fight took place. A few soldiers were on duty there; and men from various regiments were pointing out places occupied by them during the action. Squads of soldiers were eagerly hunting for (of course) something to eat, making special efforts to capture North Carolina hogs, which to a rather limited extent were found on the Island. An occasional squeal in the distance denoted a capture; and the indications were that within a short time very little "pork" would be found running around loose on Roanoke Island. I reached the barracks about dark, hungry, to be sure, and quite ready to partake of a meal of North Carolina hog and sweet potatoes."

Hunting hogs.

March 4th we had company drill for the first time since leaving Annapolis, save one or two attempts to drill on the *New York*. While drilling we noticed robins, bluebirds and sparrows in abundance. These birds stay in this locality all winter, which proves that the season cannot be very severe.

1862.

The soldiers got the idea of making briar wood pipes while we were at Roanoke, and some were very curious affairs. The roots grew in all sorts of fantastic shapes, and with a deal of skill and patience the boys made very handsome pipes for friends at home.

Briar wood.

Orders came at last for all the wounded to be sent on board the steamers for home, so they were all transferred accordingly, and we wished them good luck on their departure.

"I went one day to the hospital, a rough building erected for that purpose, to see Corporal Horace Brooks of our company. He was wounded in the foot, and lay on his cot looking quite comfortable, and talked very cheerfully. He said there were three men near him in the hospital who had but two legs among them. One had none, and two had lost one each; and a singular fact was that the one who lost both legs was doing well, while another who lost only a finger had brain fever set in and died. So it goes."

Singular case.

March 6th we went on board the "Old Wheelbarrow" or stern-wheel steamer *(Union)*, and were

1862. —— taken to the *New York*, where we occupied our old quarters again, the sergeants taking the same little state room as before, which was quite by itself and was reached from the outside. It seemed like getting home to be in our old bunks again.

On the 7th we had a regular old Hatteras gale, a gentle reminder of what had been and might be again. On the 9th it cleared away and we had a most delightful day of it. Through the winter at Hatteras it is safe to calculate on two storms a week, and not of the gentle sort, but regular tearers.

"It is strange how things are mixed in this soldier life of ours. Now everything seems like peace—waters quiet, boats gliding about in all directions, and shouts of laughter from all the vessels in our vicinity. Rumor has it that we are on the eve of another battle."

NOTE. The Captain Cole mentioned on page 78, is said to have been an officer in the famous Richmond Blues, one of the most aristocratic companies in Virginia.

CHAPTER VI.

THE CAPTURE OF NEW BERNE.

MARCH 11th we were ordered to move, but had some trouble on account of the four or five schooners we were to tow. When we got fairly under way we run aground, and the soldiers were obliged to go on board small steamers to lighten up the *New York*, and the tugs had a hard time to pull her off. All this detained us five hours. Meantime one of the sailors fell overboard, which caused a ripple of excitement, but the man swam like a fish and was picked up all right by a small boat.

The morning of March 12th found us at Hatteras near our old anchoring ground, but we started again, supposed to be bound for New Berne, ninety miles from Hatteras Inlet; and had a delightful day's sail, reaching the mouth of the Neuse River about 4 P. M., and found the rest of the fleet ready and waiting.

1862.

On the move.

1862.

Up the River.

We steamed slowly but boldly up the river, passing but few houses scattered along on either side; and noticed that the country was well wooded, and apparently more uneven than the section we had left. We anchored about 8 in the evening at a place called Slocum's Creek. We had seen during the day tall columns of dark smoke in different directions, thought by some to be signals of our approach. We did not pass a single strange sail, nothing in fact save a small sail boat containing two men, which was brought up rather suddenly by a solid shot from one of our gunboats.

Forebodings.

We had orders to land in light marching order as at Roanoke. It was evident that we had a bigger job on our hands than the affair on the Island; and "Old Posey" consoled us with the prediction that some of us would lose the number of our mess before many hours.

The Neuse River is a noble stream, between two and three miles wide at its mouth, and navigable for large vessels and steamers to New Berne. Slocum's Creek is sixteen or eighteen miles below New Berne, and about the same distance from the mouth of the Neuse.

The night passed quietly away. Going on deck about midnight the scene was an impressive one. A silence almost oppressive rested over Burnside's fleet; no lights were visible anywhere, but the forms of the vessels were plainly to be seen, and the shore on either side of the river, bordered with forest trees, lay dark and silent under the dim starlight.

1862.

Midnight scene.

On the morning of March 13th, after the woods had been shelled by the gunboats, the troops landed in much the same way as at Roanoke. Lines of boats were drawn as near the shore as possible by light-draft steamers; the boats were then separated and made for the shore. It was a singularly beautiful sight; the boats were crowded with men "Wearing the Blue," and their bayonets glistened as if tipped with sparks of sunshine. There was the same strife as at Roanoke as to who should land first; but here parts of several companies were landing at the same time, Company A among the first; and many jumped out of the boats and waded ashore. If it was a mistake on the Rebels' part in allowing us to land on Roanoke Island, here was another one. We all landed, and not an opposing shot was fired. Company A was formed quickly in the woods under live oak trees from whose branches hung long festoons

Landing of the troops.

of gray moss which waved in the slightest breeze, while vines had crept from tree to tree covering their tops completely. Birds were twittering in the branches, and we marched away from this delightful spot with scarce a thought of the terrible scenes we might pass through in the next few hours.

The Company was sent on ahead; passing some log huts and seeing no people, we halted after tramping about two miles. Soon a part of Reno's brigade passed us, with the Twenty-first in advance. In a short time the Twenty-fifth came up, and we fell in and pushed on towards New Berne through pine forests. We passed large, rough buildings that had been used as barracks by the Rebels. An old darky here told us the Rebels "run like jingo when dey knowed de Yanks was comin." It had been a cavalry station, and their scouts had seen us land, and had given the alarm, when the whole crowd left for New Berne, and in such a hurry that their saddles, bridles and other equipments lay scattered around in great confusion. They left their tables standing with breakfast scarcely touched. We stopped but a few minutes, but long enough for some of us to pretty nearly finish that breakfast. Of course we were hungry—it was certainly over an hour since we had eaten *our* breakfast—and soldiers are always hungry. It was here that McLane played a practical joke on some of us—oh Jemsy, how could you! If I remember rightly the Captain was in the scrape. McLane came out of the barracks bringing a large tin dish filled with a dark brown substance, and cried out, "*Sugar*, boys, *Sugar!*" "Here, Jemsy, here," "This way, Jemsy"; and a score of hands made a grab at the dish, a score of mouths were filled with the—sugar? No! It was salt, and villainous, dirty salt at that. What a spitting, sputtering, cursing was there! We marched on amid the shouts of those who had not tasted the *sugar*, and the curses—not loud but deep—of those who had.

1862.

Salt for sugar.

And now it came on to rain, and shortly the roads were heavy with mud. The marching became harder every hour, still there was no grumbling; and when Gen. Foster rode along and announced (false rumor by the way) that the Army of the Potomac had advanced, and that Manassas was taken, the air rung with the shouts of the soldiers. Soon we had a report from the advance that a large earthwork directly across the road we were traveling had been evacuated by the enemy. This bit of

Hard marching.

news was also received with the greatest enthusiasm, and served to keep our spirits up for the remainder of the day. We soon came in sight of the deserted battery, and were struck with its appearance. It was built at the point where the road we were traveling crossed the railroad to New Berne, and commanded both railroad and turnpike. It was intended for three heavy guns when completed. The earthworks extended from this point to the Neuse River on our right, and a good distance beyond the railroad on our left; and if these works had been properly defended we should have had a deal of trouble in getting through them.

1862.

Rebel defenses.

We pushed forward through mud and rain, with frequent halts for a few minutes rest; and at dark turned into the woods on the right of the road for a cheerless bivouac in the wet. It is not a pleasant thing to contemplate—a bivouac in a heavy rain on ground already soaked with water—for it had rained steadily for hours and there was now no cessation; but here was the place for us to stop, so there was nothing to be said about it. In spite of the rain we soon had fires started, and our coffee cooking. Haversacks were opened, and the everlasting "salt horse" and hard-tack brought forth; and these with

Bivouac.

our tin (quart) cups full of piping hot coffee sweetened just right, made us, considering all things, a good supper.

1862.

Now we looked around for some place to turn in. It was amusing to see the different ways the boys took to provide sleeping places. One man who had found two rough logs, rolled them close together and went to sleep on top of them, with his rubber blanket over him. Three or four were sitting upright together with their backs against a large tree, and their rubber blankets drawn over their heads. Others cut brush and small limbs of trees to sleep on—anything to keep them out of the wet. Some, by fastening two rubber blankets together and stretching them between trees with slant or pitch enough to shed the water, obtained a good shelter, large enough for four or more to lie under, while two more rubber blankets kept them from the wet ground. These blankets measured eight feet by four, and had eyelet holes all round the edge, being easily fastened together by strings; and it was by using them somewhat as described that the boys got the greatest benefit from them.

Bivouac in the wet.

Soldiers choose their tent-mates, and chum together at every bivouac while on a march; for instance, the officers messed together in camp and bivouac, the sergeants usually did the same, and the company was divided into squads of four or more, who were always found together in little families, so to speak. On this night the Sergeants had made a shelter, a sort of tent of rubber blankets. Having started with three days' rations we had enough to eat; and when "Jemsy" produced a candle and placed it in the end of a bayonet which he stuck in the ground inside, we felt more comfortable, for we could see just how wretched and miserable we were.

Scouting parties were sent out in different directions during the night, and guards posted; but those of us off duty managed to get some sleep, wet through as we were, overcoats and all.

We will look now at the defenses of New Berne. We had passed without hindrance through the first line of works, and a strong one it was too; and we had reason to suppose we were near the second line, as indeed we were (within half a mile). This second line was perhaps ten miles or more from the place of landing, and perhaps six miles from New Berne. It consisted of earthworks—regular intrenchments—extending from the River Neuse to the railroad, a distance of a mile; and beyond the railroad a long line of rifle pits extended half a mile further, ending with a two-gun battery on the edge of a large swamp. The works as far as the railroad were protected with a deep ditch in front, about ten feet wide and six feet deep. At the river on the enemy's left, was Fort Thompson mounting thirteen guns, some pivot that could be fired in any direction. This fort had a bomb proof, was very strong, and certainly a bad thing to approach. Three guns could sweep the field in front of the intrenchments, and ten guns commanded the river. The Neuse was blockaded by twenty or more sunken ships, a row of piles, and any number of torpedoes. Above Fort Thompson, on the river towards New Berne, was a battery of eight guns, and beyond this another of four guns, besides one or two smaller works not completed. The county road we tramped to this place passed through these fortifications about midway between the river and the railroad; and at this point was a sort of lunette mounting three guns that commanded the road and every approach thereto. The entire line of works was thoroughly built, in perfect order, and the position was an exceedingly strong one. To defend these works the

1862.

The Rebel defenses.

1862. enemy had some nine thousand men, including five hundred cavalry, with over thirty pieces of artillery. To attack and capture this position Burnside had about nine thousand men, and at the most, eight or ten small howitzers. But he had the gunboats also, which, as we shall see, did their part in the battle. The Rebels had prepared a large raft loaded with cotton, tar, turpentine and other combustibles, *Fire raft.* which was to be set on fire and floated down the river, and of course would destroy the Yankee gunboats—only it didn't. The wind blew the wrong way and it floated up against the wharf and set it on fire, and did no harm whatever to the fleet.

It was a long night, that night before the Battle of New Berne, but like all other things it had an end. The earliest daylight of the 14th found us astir, crawling around like so many half-drowned flies,—cold, wet, stiff, sore and hungry; but by moving quickly, many of us managed to get something to eat and the "cup of coffee," before the expected order "Fall in" was heard. The order was not long delayed, and we were once more on the *Opening of the Battle.* road. We had marched but a short distance, perhaps a quarter of a mile, when firing was heard ahead, which told us that the battle had opened.

25th Regt., Mass. Vols. 107

The Twenty-fifth filed into the woods on the right of the road, and with the rest of the brigade formed in line of battle, and pressed forward slowly, Company A having the right of the regiment, which had the right of the brigade, We very soon found ourselves at the edge of a clearing beyond which, at about three hundred yards distance, were the Rebel earthworks extending as far as we could see, right and left. While here Sergeant Putnam was sent out with one man (Corporal Jaalam Gates, afterwards a captain in U. S. colored troops) to reconnoiter, with orders not to fire, but as quietly as possible see what could be made out of the situation. They plunged at once into the woods and made their way towards the river. They observed the Rebel earthworks, and at last came in sight of Fort Thompson, with its guns in position to sweep the whole clearing in front of the fortifications. Making what observations they could, they were about to return when a Rebel was discovered standing on a stump, hand over his face to shade his eyes, and his rifle in the other hand. He had evidently seen our troops, for his eyes were riveted upon the spot they occupied. "I say, Sergeant," said the Corporal, "that's about a hundred yards; I can pop that fellow."

1862.
March 14

Battle of New Berne.

as I would a turkey," and he raised his rifle to do it; but the orders were not to fire, so they returned to the regiment and reported.

1862. March 14

Meantime line of battle had been formed in the edge of the woods, with the enemy's intrenchments close at hand and in plain sight, the Twenty-fifth Regiment on the extreme right. We now heard loud cheering on the left, and knew the Twenty-first was engaged. We here received the enemy's fire from the front and from Fort Thompson on the right, several of the regiment being wounded at the first fire from the fort. Our gunboats, too, having ascended the river thus far, were throwing shells over our heads, which fell short of the Rebel earthworks and burst directly in our front, fairly shaking the earth, throwing up columns of dirt, and tearing great holes in the ground at every explosion. The position was a bad one, and we were soon withdrawn and placed further to the left.

Battle of New Berne.

The fight was now raging furiously all along the line. We passed our howitzer battery of four guns; here the fight had been severe, and in all directions lay the dead and wounded of the battery. Bullets were flying around thick, and solid shot came crashing through the trees. The excitement at this time was very great,—firing along the whole line, and loud cheering away down the left where the gallant Twenty-first had made a charge, entered the enemy's works and were driven out, but had re-formed, charged and entered the works again, this time to *stay*. We, also, were ordered to charge, and with a wild hurrah we started at double-quick, and in about as short a time as it takes to write it, our boys were swarming over the Rebel works like bees; and the colors of the Twenty-fifth were planted in the battery. It was claimed that our state colors were the first that floated over the enemy's intrenchments. The distance where the charge was made between the woods and the earthworks was about two hundred yards; and we had but just started when a solid shot—evidently from Fort Thompson —came tearing along, struck a tree on our right, glanced, and going through the ranks of Company A, killed comrade Eli Pike. The shot struck him in the side and mangled him shockingly. We could not stop; one glance, as we passed over him—a quivering, bleeding mass of humanity—was the last we saw of Eli Pike, the *first* of Company A to die on the battle field.

1862. March 14

Battle of New Berne.

Death of Eli Pike.

It was a horrible sight as we entered the enemy's works—dead and dying men, dead and dying horses, in every conceivable position, some alone, others in little heaps of two or three, all smeared with blood and begrimed with powder and dirt. Many, perhaps most, of the Rebels, were shot in the head. We noticed a dead Rebel soldier, seated on a log, his rifle beside him, and his back supported against a tree. He had been shot in the act of eating a piece of bread; the mouthful bitten off remained between his teeth, while the right hand still holding the loaf was raised to his lips. Death had come like a flash, and his limbs were rigid in an instant. This was a very singular case.

1862. March 14

Battle of New Berne.

The enemy were now in full retreat towards New Berne, a portion of one regiment marching off in good order, with colors flying; but the road, as was the case at Roanoke, was strewn with guns and equipments thrown away in the hasty flight. Our regiment formed soon after, and Company A was sent to skirmish through the woods towards the railroad, which we did, capturing many prisoners, then following the railroad towards New Berne, where were crowds of Rebels flying to the city.

Retreat of the enemy.

25th Regt., Mass. Vols.

On either side were seen many of the enemy making signs which indicated their desire to surrender.

1862.

Gen. Foster on horseback rode along with Company A as we pushed on towards the town. We soon noticed a huge column of black smoke rising high over New Berne, and saw at once that the Rebels had set the city on fire—a Moscow on a small scale! We soon reached the Trent River, and found the railroad bridge, some fifteen hundred feet long, in flames and rapidly going to destruction. We stopped but a short time on the banks of the Trent, and then crossed over in small steamers and took possession of the town. The gunboats all this time had been fighting their way up the river, reaching the town before the troops, and were assisting in putting out the fires.

We enter New Berne.

So ended the Battle of New Berne, with a loss to the Twenty-fifth Regiment of twenty-six killed and wounded. Our Company had one man killed. The total Union loss was one hundred killed and about five hundred wounded. We captured several hundred prisoners, thousands of muskets, thirty pieces of artillery, and a large quantity of ammunition. The Rebel loss in killed and wounded is not known, but probably it was less than ours.

CHAPTER VII.

NEW BERNE AND CAMP OLIVER.

1862.

Our quarters.

THE BUILDING in New Berne occupied by Company A was known as the Merchants' Bank, and was located on Craven street. The door was locked, but the axes of the pioneers had opened it, and we were at once in comfortable quarters. The building had been cleaned out, but we had a nice shelter, and it was a striking contrast to the last few days,—one night we bivouac in the woods in mud and rain, the next we are in a brick house in town, sleeping on mattresses *borrowed* from the neighbors. This is the ebb and flow of a soldier's life—famine one day, feast the next.

Tired out as we were with the work of the last few days, we were glad of a chance to rest. This battle of New Berne was fought on Friday. We also landed at Roanoke on a Friday—unlucky days for somebody, but not for us.

"Saturday morning found us all right, and after breakfast there was a general scouting around for —of course—something to eat; and the result of this still hunting was a dinner—shall I describe it? Turkeys, two kinds, boiled and stewed; hot biscuit and butter; and—tell it not—syrup, preserved peaches and honey. How did we do it? The boys of Company A were always in luck. We found one room in the bank building which was locked; we opened it, and found it was the store-room of the family that had resided in the building. Here were all sorts of preserved fruit in goodly quantities,— peaches, tamarinds, berries, etc.; and the "scouts" brought in butter, flour, turkeys, and a solitary chicken."

1862.

Our first dinner.

We enjoyed now, for a short time, the poetry of soldiering,—comfortable quarters and duty light. It seemed strange to wander about the streets of the captured city; all was new to northern eyes. Most of the houses were abandoned, but some were left with the oldest slaves, while the younger and most valuable ones had been taken away. Streets deserted and silent, save when the stillness was broken by the tramp of the soldier, the citizens— those who remained—keeping inside their houses.

1862.   Black faces peered at us from all quarters, and pieces of white cloth waved from every corner and Negro shanty. The slaves did not appear to be afraid of the soldiers, although they had been taught to fear us.

The soldiers and sailors had free run in New Berne for the first twenty-four hours, and then the place settled down in peace and quiet under military rule. Of course there was more or less pillaging, but little harm was done; indeed the Union soldiers saved the place from destruction by fire at the hands of its citizens and the Rebel soldiery. The people left New Berne in a perfect panic, and the streets

Effects of the panic. and roads were covered with all sorts of property— household goods, clothing, wagons, and such like. A beautiful piano was found in one street, and soon after it might have been seen in the soldiers' quarters, the *music* taken out, and horses feeding from the case.

"I noticed a pleasant-looking house one day when on guard, and found it no exception to the general rule—it was deserted, and nearly everything of value had been carried away. There were several horses in the stable and cows in the field. A few slaves stood around looking in stupid wonder at the strange visitors. 'Massa's goned away,' they said. I went over the house; a piano with a pile of sheet music, a poodle dog, a cage of canaries, and a large cat, indicated refinement and taste; but now desolation had swept over everything. On the opposite side of the road was a large vineyard; a few weeks later Fort Totten had sprung up there and the vineyard had disappeared. It would have been wiser for the owners to have stayed on the premises and taken the oath of allegiance, for then they would have been protected; but this shows how great was their fright."

1862.

Negroes began to come in from the country around, some from Goldsboro,' who reported no fortifications between that place and New Berne; but "dey is makin some." It would seem that then was the time to have cleaned out the enemy as far as Goldsboro.'

Negroes.

The Rebels were very thoughtful in one way certainly, for they had a train of cars all ready in case of disaster to their army, and it worked very nicely for them, for the train went through New Berne in a hurry, crowded with soldiers skedaddling from the Boys in Blue.

Guard duty was about all there was for us to do for awhile; orders were very strict, and after a certain hour at night all persons found without passes were to be arrested, so it made a deal of work. One night three or four sailors were brought into the guard-house drunk, one nearly insensible. This one died before morning in consequence of his debauch.

We saw here for the first time women and children practicing the disgusting habit of snuff dipping. A small stick was dipped into a snuff box and the end is then rubbed over the teeth and gums, talking while the operation is going on, the stick protruding from the mouth.

"A visit to the battle ground gave us a better idea of the strength of the fortifications, and of the work performed in the late battle. There were over twenty vessels in the blockade, mostly schooners and brigs, and some appeared to be new. Mounting the breastwork we walked from Fort Thompson on the Neuse River to the railroad, a distance of one and a half miles without a break, save where the county road passed through. The position was a very strong one, and upon first thought it seems as if it could have been held; but the gunboats settled the matter by breaking the blockade, and flanking the enemy's works, furnishing material aid in the capture of New Berne."

1862.

March 25th, our building being wanted for a hospital, our officers selected for company quarters another brick house on Johnston street, furnished with marble chimney pieces, mirrors, and a clock, and surrounded with a large garden, with flowers and peach trees in bloom. It was in a fine neighborhood, quiet and retired—who wouldn't be a soger! We found an old cooking stove in the cellar, and set it up. Warm biscuit, baked beans, etc. followed. Company A was always in luck.

Sunday, March 30th, the whole regiment turned out and marched to church. It was a curious sight —pews filled with Blue Coats and glittering bayonets, six soldiers and six rifles to a pew, darkies peering in at doors and windows, the star spangled banner in one corner, while Chaplain James in the pulpit completed the picture.

At church.

At this time troops were coming into New Berne in large numbers, and camps were forming all about. The Twenty-fifth Regiment had been the first to enter the city, headed by Company A.

The city of New Berne is situated at the junction of the Neuse and Trent rivers, and is prettily laid out, with streets straight and wide and completely shaded with large trees. The gardens of New Berne, when properly cared for, must have made the place an earthly·paradise. An endless variety of flowers could be found here, and the floral procession continued, seemingly, all through the year. Beautiful birds made music among the trees, and at night the mocking bird tuned his varied lays. Nature had scattered here her benefits in lavish profusion, and grim war with all its terrors could not neutralize her power. The city contained about twelve hundred white inhabitants at the time of its capture.

In the latter part of March, Major McCafferty resigned, and our Captain was promoted to be Major of the Regiment, First Lieutenant Frank E. Goodwin being advanced to the command of the Company. In consequence of this change Company A became the eighth in line, instead of holding the *right* of the Regiment, a position we had been proud of. It was rather disheartening. Officers go up, companies go down—in rank. We talked the matter over in our quarters. Had not he led us in two victories? Had not we achieved honor and a name under his command? So we concluded to promote him—our pony Captain—to be Major;

but the trouble did not end here, for in October following Lieutenant-Colonel Sprague resigned, and soon after Colonel Upton did likewise, which left Major Pickett in command of the Twenty-fifth Regiment as Colonel. So we promoted him again, and we thought the eagles looked better on his shoulders than the captain's bars. Nor was this all; at his muster-out, in January, 1865, he was breveted Brigadier-General; and although Company A was mustered out the preceding October, still we rejoiced at his promotion.

1862.

Colonel Pickett.

On the 9th of May the Regiment left New Berne and went on picket duty at the Red House, a place we became very familiar with, as well as with Old Bogey, the owner, before we left New Berne. This place was about nine miles from New Berne, and half-way between the Neuse and Trent rivers.

By noon the Regiment was on the ground, and Camp Bullock was formed, named in honor of Hon. Alexander H. Bullock, of Worcester, Mass. Here Sibley tents took the place of our old A tents. On the 13th, a scouting party under Col. Upton, visited the place called Tuscarora, four or five miles distant. The enemy had an outpost here, and they fled on

Camp Bullock.

1862.

Expeditions.

—— our approach, setting fire to a mill before they departed. The expedition was of no great account, except in giving us experience in the sort of work we should have to do in North Carolina.

On the 15th of May the Regiment left Camp Bullock, and marched towards Trenton. We had with us the Seventeenth Massachusetts, some of the Third New York Cavalry (seven companies), and the Third Rhode Island Artillery. The cavalry had all the fighting, losing two men and killing eight or ten of the enemy, while the infantry marched there and back, twenty-five miles, without firing a shot.

Denny, in his "Wearing the Blue," relates the comical story of Bogey's old white mare alarming the pickets. The plantation of Mr. Bogey was surrounded by woods, and contained perhaps twenty acres. It was situated at the cross roads, one leading to New Berne, one to Tuscarora, and one to Bachellor's Creek.

Camp Oliver.

On the 25th of May the Regiment left the Red House and marched back to New Berne, where Camp Oliver was formed, supposed to be named in honor of Gen. H. K. Oliver, Adjutant-General of Massachusetts.

The extensive pine forests which cover a great part of eastern North Carolina, furnished the principal supply of the tar, turpentine and rosin of commerce. The forests are almost entirely destitute of birds, and in their depths the stillness is actually oppressive; and so dense is their growth that the rays of the sun, even at noonday, can scarcely penetrate the sombre shade. A pine forest is a lonely world at its best; it lacks entirely the characteristics of other forests,—the variety of leaves, the fragrant undergrowth of bush and shrub, the different forms of the trees—all these are wanting. It is monotonous and the eye tires of it. It has not the cheerful look of other forests; and while the wind rustles merrily among other trees, it moans and sighs through the pines. It affected the spirits of the men in marching through them; lively and gay as the boys usually were, they soon became sober and quieted down very much while passing through these dismal shades.

1862.

Pine forests.

The weather through the month of June was very warm, but the 4th of July was cool and comfortable. We had an eloquent oration delivered in a church by Chaplain Horace James. He compared the Rebellion of '76 with that of '61. At night we had

July 4th.

—— a big bonfire in our camp, and all the regimental bands united gave us music. The usual salutes were fired morning and evening. So passed our 4th of July.

1862.

July 25th an expedition was made to Trenton again, the Twenty-fifth and Twenty-seventh Massachusetts with Belger's Rhode Island Battery composing the detachment. We returned to New Berne the next day. August 6th, another expedition went out from New Berne on a scout, and returned on the 7th.

Expeditions.

The latter part of August our Regimental Band was discharged. This was regretted by all. We had the best band in the department, and the loss was felt by the whole body of troops in New Berne. From this time the Regiment had drums and fifes only.

Band discharged.

Thus life in New Berne glided away, and the summer of 1862 passed quickly and pleasantly. So far the health of the Company had been good, though many of the boys had been troubled with chills and fever; but no malady of a serious nature had appeared. Recruits had been coming in to the Regiment, and Company A had received its share of first rate men, and we were glad to see them.

We had fruit in abundance at New Berne—figs, persimmons, grapes, melons, etc.—all good; apples, too, but none like those of New England. Sweet potatoes were abundant.

1862.

At the rear of Camp Oliver was a large swamp in which was a considerable body of water. There were a few trees growing there. It was a pleasant sight to see wild ducks swimming about in this swamp so near us. One morning we saw eleven white cranes on one tree, presenting a very curious sight. No one was allowed to fire at them, and they appeared as unconcerned as if they were in the wilderness.

Novel sights.

David Bigelow and Charley Bartlett, wounded at Roanoke, had returned to the Company, and were now on duty as usual.

August 20th found Company A on picket at the so called Harrison House, some four or five miles from New Berne. We were accompanied by Company C. The camp here was known as Camp Inge. Life on picket was vastly more pleasant than the ordinary round of camp duty—there was more freedom and less irksome (though necessary) drill, with just danger enough to give a sort of fascination to it, and keep the boys wide awake. The picket camp

Picket duty.

1862.

—— was about half a mile in the rear of the picket lines, and was fixed up as comfortable as could be. The boys made tables, stools, and bough houses, and built ovens; washed their clothes and did their mending; read, wrote, smoked, played cards, etc.; but were ready for a "Fall in, A" at any moment. The picket guard was relieved every morning from the camp. Unless there was danger in so doing, the boys on picket duty built fire enough to cook their coffee and make themselves comfortable, a constant vigilance of course being kept up. Generally there were three men on each post, and one constantly on guard. As night comes on no fires are allowed, and when darkness covers the scene the objects so familiar by daylight assume a different look—as one of the boys expressed it: "The stumps begin to walk, and everything moves." The soldier on his lonely post will be startled by sounds he would not notice by daylight—the snapping of a twig near him, or the tread of some wild animal, will keep him wide awake; and often, when no wind is stirring, a tree will fall with a tremendous crash that will awaken the echoes of the forest. Again, the wind rises, and the woods so still before are now filled with new and strange sounds; or perhaps

Picket duty.

a storm comes on, and with getting chilled and drenched with rain, the night drags slowly away; but morning comes at last, and with it the ever welcome relief.

The picket line extended from the Neuse to the Trent rivers, and all were anxious to be "out on picket." It was when on such duty that Charley Knowlton caught the deer. Charley had heard the darkies say they had "seen deer run in dese ere woods"; and at once visions of venison steak flitted across his imagination, and he soon, with some assistance, slyly dug a pit in the path in which the deer were supposed to run, and carefully covered it. For several days nothing disturbed the pit, but one morning early he found the game was caught, but it was a poor, sick cavalry horse. There he was, sticking his nose out of the pit. What was to be done?—they could not get him out, and it would not do to let him remain where he was. So Charley —full of expedients—shot the poor old horse, and buried him in the pit he had dug for the deer. There is more than one way—even out of a pit.

One day while at Camp Inge a severe thunder storm came up; the boys off duty were lying listlessly in their tents, their rifles in a circle around

1862.

Knowlton and his deer pit.

each center pole. A sharp flash of lightning came with a loud clap of thunder, and struck in the camp, killing a horse. Part of the bolt went down one of the tent poles, scattered the rifles in every direction, but did no harm to the boys in the tent. This was only an *incident* in a soldier's life.

1862.

An incident.

Noon of September 23rd found Company A again at Camp Oliver. At night fires were built in the company streets—a sanitary measure—and we turned in at "taps," tired, but a merry lot of soldiers.

On the 24th of September Comrade Lucius F. Kingman died of diptheria after a few days' illness. He was a noble fellow—kind hearted, pleasant, and a true soldier. He was buried at New Berne.

Some months before, just after the Battle of Roanoke, Comrade Thomas Earle, somewhat to the surprise of the other members, left the Company on a furlough, and went back to Massachusetts; and great was the astonishment when, after the Battle of New Berne, he returned a *lieutenant* in the same company he had left thirty days before as a private soldier. It was rather galling to the rest, but *queer* things happen in the army frequently. It would seem almost as a rule that commissions were not won in the field, but obtained through influence

A promotion

at home. September 1, Lieutenant Earle resigned —a privilege officers have; privates, if I remember rightly, do not have that privilege—and this brought about other changes in the Company. "Old Posey" became Second Lieutenant, and Burr, or "Birdie" was made Orderly Sergeant, the vacancies in the Sergeants' ranks being filled by others.

1862.

It may be well, in this place to give a list of the boys of "Old Company A" who received commissions. It will be seen that some were commissioned in other regiments; but, while we did not like to part with old faces, we rejoiced at the good fortune of those who obtained promotion, and we regarded it as additional honor to the Company.

LIST OF PROMOTIONS OF CO. A MEN.

Captain Josiah Pickett, to Maj. and Col. 25th; Bv. Brig.-Gen.

Promotions.

First Lieut. F. E. Goodwin, to Capt.

Second Lieut. M. B. Bessey, to 1st Lt. & Capt.

Orderly Sergeant G. A. Johnson, to Second Lieut.

Sergeant Geo. Burr, to First Lieut.

Sergeant J. J. McLane, to Second Lieut. 1st N. C. Union Vols.

1862.

Promotions.

Corporal Jaalam Gates, to Capt. U. S. Colored Troops.
Corporal John A. Chenery, to First Lieut and Adjutant, 1st N. C. Union Vols.
Corporal Lewis J. Elwell, to Sergeant Major.
Private Thomas Earle, to Second Lieut.
Private James M. Hervey, to First Lieut. N. C. Union Vols.
Private John L. Goodwin, to 1st Lt., 57th Mass.
Private C. L. Hutchins, to Lieut. U. S. Vols.
Private S. W. Phillips, to First Lieut. U. S. Colored Troops.
Private Henry W. Reed, to Signal Corps.
Private Geo. L. Seagrave, to First Lieut. U. S. Colored Troops.
Private Hiram Staples, to Signal Corps.
Private Augustus Stone, to Second Lieut., 4th Mass. Heavy Artillery.
Private Julius M. Tucker, to First Lieut., 57th Mass.
Private Hale Wesson, to Signal Corps.
Private C. B. Kendall, to Lieut., Adj. & Capt.
Private Sylvanus Bullock, to Lieut. U. S. Vols.
Private T. M. Ward, to 1st Lieut. and Capt.
Private Edwin A. Morse, to Lieut. 36th Mass.

September 15th the Regiment left New Berne with other troops on transport steamers, and after a delightful day's sail through Pamlico and Albemarle Sounds, passing Roanoke Island on the way, reached Plymouth, at the mouth of the Roanoke River. The object intended was an invasion of the interior of the State, but that being abandoned, we returned to New Berne, having enjoyed a fine excursion of over four hundred miles.

1862.

Colonel Upton left for home October 28. Ill health and other considerations compelled him to sever his connection with the Regiment, to the regret both of himself and his command. An elegant sword, which cost one thousand dollars, was presented to him by the private soldiers of the Regiment, as a token of their esteem.

Resignation of Col. Upton.

CHAPTER VIII.

EXPEDITIONS.

1862.

Fun with the darkies.

ON THE 30th of October six companies of the Regiment left New Berne in light marching order, and going on board transports, sailed for Washington, N. C., one hundred miles distant. During our brief stay at this place Company A was quartered in a large tobacco warehouse; and for amusement, squads were sent out to pick up negroes and bring them to the quarters, where they were made to show their agility in dancing. One old darky was brought in, a ring formed around him, and he was told to dance. "But I'se got de rheumatiz," he said. "Never mind, you must dance," and the boys struck up a low, monotonous tune, keeping time by patting their hands on their knees. The old fellow began to dance slowly and clumsily at first, but as he warmed up he threw off his jacket and shook his heels as lively as a boy, the soldiers shouting, "Go it, rheumatiz," "Sail in, old rheumatics," "Go it while you're young," and the like. The old man appeared to enjoy it as well as the boys, and when he became tired he put on his old ragged coat, and walked away laughing heartily. Another negro was brought in—a young fellow. "I can't dance for you, sogers," "Suppose you try," said one of the boys. "I can't, I'se religious." "The h—l you are," said one. "Does it hurt you much?" said another. "What church do you belong to?" asked the third. "I'se a Methodis," he responded. "Let him go, boys," said the Sergeant, and he walked quietly away. Another was brought in, struggling violently with the soldiers, who were trying to pacify him by telling him no harm was intended. Once in the ring, he looked wildly around, then making a sudden spring he broke through the crowd and ran like a deer, amid the shouts of the boys.

When we reached Washington the artillery and cavalry coming overland from New Berne had not arrived, and we were obliged to wait for them. Col. Pickett said he did not wish to confine the men to quarters while in Washington, but would give them the run of the town. There was to be no rioting or pillaging; he expected they would behave like men, and that, at the sound of the drum, every one would be in his place. Guns were stacked, sentinels posted, and the boys scattered to seek such amusement as they thought best. We have seen how Company A boys amused themselves. It was some three hours or more before the other troops arrived, but at the first sound of the drum the men came trooping from all directions, and before it ceased beating every one was in place, and every gun taken when the order "take arms" was given. The Colonel was much pleased, and complimented the boys on their promptness.

1862.

We left Sunday morning, November 2nd, marching through a thinly settled country, the Twenty-fifth having the tedious duty of guarding the baggage train. About the middle of the afternoon the advance (Forty-fourth Mass., nine months' men) met the enemy and had a skirmish, with a small loss to the Union troops, the cavalry and artillery doing most of the fighting. This skirmish took place at an extensive swamp through which flowed a considerable stream of water that crossed the road we were traveling; at this point was the fighting, and we passed several dead Rebels, one rolled in his

Tarboro' march.

blanket, with his head bound up. Broken cannon also lay here. We soon after bivouacked for the night. This place was called Rawl's Mill.

Early morning saw us again on the road, and marching through a much better country. Williamston, on the Roanoke River, was reached about noon. This was a pretty village of ten or twelve hundred inhabitants. We halted here until 4 P. M., and in the meantime set about getting something to eat as usual. Our foragers were very successful, and brought in a variety of food. For instance, we had beef, hog, sheep, chickens—all just killed, and salt horse. Soldiers say, "Live to-day if you die to-morrow." We were marching through a good country and lived accordingly.

The march was resumed, the route turning for a few miles towards Hamilton, and by 10 P. M. we again went into bivouac. Sunrise next morning found us once more on the road, and our march was through woods at times on fire both sides of the way. At noon we came to a more open country, near what is known as Rainbow Bluff. It was understood we might have trouble here, but we found no opposition. This bluff, forty or fifty feet above the water, had been strongly fortified, and com-

1862.

—— manded the river, but the enemy had disappeared. We found our gunboats at this point; they were to ascend the river while we continued our march towards Hamilton. This place, another pretty village of a few hundred people, was reached about 3 P. M., and we had a rest, with a "good square meal," until 6 o'clock, when we heard the order "Fall in." Thus far the country was much better than around New Berne.

During our halt near Williamston we found with other plunder, a number of square wooden bee hives. Quicker than it could be spoken the hives were burst open and the contents distributed among the boys. Ludicrous sight—a score of soldiers eating honey in the comb like so much bread and butter. Comrade Goulding found here in a house a small cask partly filled with wine. The darkies said it was "de church wine for de communion." "The d—l," said Goulding, "you bet it belongs to Company A now, the best way you can cook it"; and I think it did, for Company A disposed of it. In bringing it to the bivouac fire he had shaken it up so much that it was roiled and did not look clear and inviting. He offered some to Captain Goodwin, who looked at it, smelled of it, and finally tasted it. "Goulding,

Communion wine

it will *kill* you to drink that stuff." "Happy death!" said Goulding, as he swallowed a generous allowance of the *stuff*. He survived.

1862.

At about 10 P. M. we left Hamilton in flames, supposed to have been set by the sailors. Some thought our own boys were responsible for it. Be that as it may, we marched from the town by the light of its burning houses. It was a wild sight— crowds of sailors and soldiers marching through the burning streets; bayonets glistening, flames roaring, and timbers crashing. This was war.

Burning of Hamilton

The next day's march was a long and tedious one. We started at early dawn, and, with only occasional halts, marched till midnight, when we bivouacked in a cornfield within a short distance of the railroad leading to Tarboro'. We were thoroughly exhausted, and, pulling up the dry corn stalks and laying them thickly between the rows, made quite comfortable beds. A cold northeast storm set in during the night, but we slept soundly in spite of it. "I remember being awakened by rain dashing in my face, and feeling about for my cap, which had fallen from my head, found it half full of water." It was a cold and cheerless time.

Discomfort.

1862.

Trains were heard running very often during the night, and scouts reported that soldiers by thousands were pouring into Tarboro'. In consequence of this information it was decided that an attack upon the place would be bad policy, and, after a halt of some hours, we commenced a retreat. On this march Negroes by hundreds followed us into Plymouth.

On the retreat. We passed through Hamilton again, this time in a heavy snow storm, and we now regretted the burning of the town. A few Negro cabins were all that remained of that pretty village. We stayed here all night, and then pushed on to Williamston; the roads were in horrible condition, with snow and mud several inches deep, and many of the boys' shoes were in bad shape. Walter Richards ("Shucks," as we called him) actually marched miles barefooted, until we found a pair of shoes for him. We approached Plymouth, on the Roanoke river, but found the bridge destroyed, so we bivouacked for the night while the pioneers reconstructed it.

The march for the last few days had been very severe, but the boys boiled their coffee, ate their supper, smoked their pipes, talked over the events of the day, rolled themselves in their blankets, and soon—save the sentries' tread as they paced their beats—all was quiet around the bivouac fires. "I was about to roll myself in my blanket when Jimmy Wesson touched me on the arm and said: 'Come out here, I can give you a *better room* than this'; and following him a short distance I found, to my surprise, a bed made up, with a fire close by— feather bed, sheets, blankets, white pillows, and everything in nice order. 'Turn in here with me; I reckon it's all right.' It was quite an inducement, but I preferred to sleep by the fire." Soldiers make the best of the situation, and why should they not? Where did the bed come from? *Borrowed*, of course, from some house on the road. On these expeditions soldiers took what they wanted wherever it was to be found, except from houses occupied, where the soldiers were treated civilly. Probably nine-tenths of the Southern people would have been better off if they had stayed at home and tried to take care of their property, taking the oath of allegiance.

In the morning (Nov. 10) we crossed the bridge and entered Plymouth. The Twenty-fifth and the Twenty-seventh, with some cavalry, remained here, but most of the troops left at once for New Berne. We had comfortable quarters in a house, but as we had no extra clothing and the nights were cold, we

1862.

Wesson's bed.

1862.

Plymouth.

—— suffered some until our blankets were sent on from New Berne. Plymouth was a very pretty town of some twelve hundred inhabitants, with two churches, a hotel, court house, jail, pillory, and whipping post. The latter the boys of Company A tipped over and smashed. The streets were shaded with large elm trees, as those of many Southern villages were. Many trees were covered with English ivy hanging in long festoons from their branches. We feasted on persimmons while here. This fruit was new to most of us; it is a sort of date plum, and is not palatable until touched or mellowed by frost; it then becomes soft and agreeable to the taste. They were much sought for by the boys during our stay in Plymouth. Grapes, sweet potatoes, and corn we also had in abundance.

Deceiving the miller.

There was a miller in Plymouth, and the soldiers would forage for provisions and bring in, with other stuff, lots of corn, and the miller would grind it for them. This was very good. But the miller had a large lot of corn stored in his mill, and, as the grain became scarce outside, some of the soldiers managed slyly to get at the miller's store, and would steal corn from one end of the mill and carry it around to the other, and have the miller grind it, he taking meal for pay. This trick worked nicely for a short time, but it was discovered by the miller at last, and I am quite sure he did not pray for us, although he was a very good man. Thus, by this simple process, we kept the miller busy, and had fresh ground meal for ourselves. Soldiers are full of expedients, and this was one.

The Union men in Plymouth had formed a company of soldiers. We called them "Buffaloes," and they did some good service. Some of our boys received commissions in these "Buffalo" companies; and all agree that they made good soldiers, and were Union-loving men.

Buffaloes.

On this Tarboro' march, the Forty-fourth Massachusetts Regiment—nine months' men who had received quite large bounties—was the best clothed regiment in the expedition. The march proved severe for its men, and many of them threw away their overcoats, which were very nice ones. Our boys "gobbled" them at once, and when we reached our old camp at New Berne we were much better off in the way of overcoats than when we left.

Discarded overcoats.

On the return march from Hamilton, Jimmy Wesson picked up an old two-wheeled mule cart with mule attached. Jimmy was always very dis-

1862.

Wesson's mule cart.

interested; and this cart would be such a nice thing for the boys, to carry the overcoats and blankets of those who had them, and to help the tired ones by giving them a ride. He soon had a load, and it worked well. Just then three or four of the Forty-fourth boys came along pretty well used up, and in spite of all protests, mounted the cart. Jimmy quietly got down to "fix the harness a bit," and he did fix it. Suddenly up went the thills and over went the cart backwards, tipping out blankets and overcoats, and laying the Forty-fourth men sprawling in the dust. They picked themselves up and beat a retreat amid roars of laughter. Willing hands helped to reload the cart, and Jimmy rode on in triumph. Now when we reached Plymouth, and the boys thankfully received their overcoats from the cart, the vehicle was found to be more than half filled with the private plunder of this same disinterested Jimmy.

Death of Waters.

While in Plymouth we heard of the death of Comrade Edwin D. Waters, of Company A. He was a fine soldier and a noble-hearted fellow. He hailed from Millbury, and was about twenty-six years old. Some thought he actually died from getting low-spirited and discouraged about the war. No doubt many soldiers did die from this cause alone. Waters was in the hospital at New Berne at the time of his death.

While occupying Plymouth, Captain Parkhurst was acting Provost Marshal, Colonel Pickett being in command. On this march we had no clothes aside from those on our backs, and as weeks went by, we got into a pretty bad condition. We were ragged, dirty and—the word must be said—lousy. So we concluded to have a washing day, every man to be his own washerwoman. Fires were built in the rear of the house we occupied, kettles procured, and at it we went. We took off all the clothes we could possibly spare, and thrust them into the kettles of boiling water to kill the graybacks (vermin), and after some time boiling, gave them a thorough washing. Meantime a comical sight presented itself— soldiers moving about trying to keep warm, wearing an airy costume for the season—army cap, overcoat, and brogans,—"Only these and nothing more"; but we came out victorious, for we beat the graybacks.

Many people came into Plymouth from the country while we were there, coming often many miles down the river in dugouts—a kind of canoe made from a single log. These people were both whites

We become lousy.

—— and blacks, and were seeking protection under the starry flag.

1862.

Thanksgiving day found us still at Plymouth, Company A on guard. Some were posted on board the schooner *Skirmisher* to guard prisoners. We kept up the time-honored custom as best we could in old North Carolina, and so had a chicken dinner. When we reached Plymouth our wagon train had increased much in length, and was over four miles long.

Thanksgiving day

We left Plymouth on December 8th, passing down the Roanoke River, which is a narrow but deep stream, into the Sound past Roanoke Island, and reached New Berne about 3 P. M. of the 10th; and were ordered off again at 7 A. M. of the 11th. This was soldiering. We had been absent from New Berne nearly six weeks, had traveled a distance of over four hundred miles, and actually marched one hundred and twenty-five miles.

Return to New Berne.

Immediately on our reaching camp the cooks were set to work to cook rations for the expedition of the following day. This is always the first step in preparing for a march—to get the rations ready. Little time was there for the ordinary camp gossip and fun, but what time we had was used to the best advantage in putting our shoes and clothing in good order, overhauling our rifles and equipments, looking into knapsacks, and making everything shipshape. A soldier's rifle is supposed to be always ready. For the first time in six weeks we had an opportunity to change our shirts.

1862.

Large numbers of troops had been gathered in New Berne during our absence, so that when the expedition started, on the morning of December 11th, it comprised four brigades commanded by General Wessels, and Colonels Amory, Stevenson and Lee. These brigades were made up of twenty regiments, of which twelve were Massachusetts men. The Ninth New Jersey accompanied us as an independent organization. Belger's Rhode Island Battery and portions of other batteries were with the column, making all told probably twenty thousand men, and thirty or more pieces of artillery.* The expedition was commanded by General Foster.

Goldsboro' Expedition.

When we started at early daylight of the 11th there was a heavy fog, but it cleared away in an hour or two. We took the old road to Deep Gully, beyond which we found the way badly blockaded.

*The column on this Goldsboro' Expedition, including all the troops, with the wagons necessary for ammunition and supplies, ambulances, etc., could not have been less than six miles in length.

1862.

Heavy trees had been felled across the road for a long distance, showing that the enemy had been busy. The pioneers had a hard job cutting a road through this blockade, and after a march of a dozen miles from New Berne we bivouacked for the night. We had now frosty nights, and in spite of the many camp fires, we suffered from the cold.

A hard march.

The march of the following day (Dec. 12) was slow and tedious in the extreme—roads much obstructed and bridges destroyed—so we made even less progress than the day before. As we passed in the early evening the bright fires of the regiments already in bivouac, we thought our day's march was near its end, but not so, for we pushed on, and not till after midnight did we come to a halt. Saturday, the 13th, the march was resumed, and at a place called Southwest Creek the enemy made a stand, but were driven after a smart engagement, in which Wessels's Brigade, the Ninth New Jersey and the Twenty-third Massachusetts took part. This was within five or six miles of Kinston. Our bivouac this night was wretched and uncomfortable enough, —the ground cold and wet, and no fires allowed.

Sunday, the 14th, after a short march, it appeared that the enemy was determined to make a decided stand. The brigade of Wessels was again engaged, together with the Seventeenth, Twenty-third, Twenty-fifth and Forty-fifth Massachusetts, and the Ninth New Jersey. The cannonading was very heavy, as was also the musketry firing; and we knew, as we lay on the ground waiting for our turn to go in, that the struggle was a fierce one. Soon the wounded began to be brought to the rear, and we had full benefit of the sight as the grim procession passed close by us, still the boys chatted gaily as they talked over the situation. "How does it go?" asked one of our men of a soldier who was assisting in bringing out the wounded. "We are driving them" was the reply; and we all sprung to our feet as we heard the order, "Fall in Twenty-fifth." We moved rapidly into the woods, and noticed on either side of the way the ground thickly dotted with the bodies of the Blue and the Gray.

At this time the enemy had again fallen back, and on getting through the woods we halted near an old weather-beaten, dismal-looking building, said to be a church. Parties were detailed to bury the dead; Lieutenant Tew appeared to have command. He approached near where we were, with two men bearing a stretcher, and stopped to pick up a dead

1862.

Dec. 14. *Battle of Kinston.*

Johnny (Rebel). The body was placed on the stretcher, one arm projecting over the side. The Lieutenant bent the arm over the body, when it immediately returned to its first position. Again he replaced it and again it moved back as before. The Lieutenant looked a bit provoked, but tried it the third time with the same result. He straightened up, and with a look that meant business, exclaimed, "By G—d, Johnny, I *can* fix you," and thrust the offending hand into the jacket of the dead Rebel. This time it stayed, and the stretcher moved on.

1862.

A stubborn Rebel.

Shallow trenches, not much over two feet deep, were dug, and side by side the dead were placed therein, their faces covered, and as carefully as possible the earth was hastily thrown over them, and the order given to fall in. This may seem hard—as one of our boys expressed it: "It's kind o' rough, ain't it fellers?" But there was no other way —nothing else could be done under the circumstances; so we marched on and left them in their— is the next word GLORY?

Hasty burials.

We reached the Neuse River, fairly overlooking the town of Kinston. A bridge was here, and it was said that General Foster sent a flag of truce demanding a surrender. Rebel General Evans did not see it in that light and politely declined the honor. Foster ordered up a battery and threw shells clear over the town; the enemy departed, and we crossed the bridge and occupied the place. The Twenty-fifth bivouacked near the river in an open field. Fires were built, but first we had to get the fence rails. "As a cold kitten makes for a warm brick, so does a cold and hungry soldier go for dry fence rails." (A soldier's proverb, and a very true one.) We took fences and tore down buildings for firewood, cooked our coffee, ate our supper of hard-tack, salt horse and sweet potatoes roasted in the ashes, and then went visiting to look over the property and see what we could find. Until a late hour that night the boys were returning to the bivouac fire bringing all sorts of stuff to eat and drink. This seemed to be a great wine country, and we got hold of some very good wine, and apple jack or apple brandy, a more plebeian drink but quite passable. We found sweet potatoes in any quantity, and one goose—mighty tough it was too, after hours of boiling. We also found much tobacco.

There was a fire in Kinston that night, and no one seemed to know how it came about. Did Goulding know?

1862.

As we would have to march early in the morning there was no way to carry the eatables, so they were cooked at once, and we ate the eatables and drank the drinkables, and so settled that little matter in the quickest way. Now there was, strictly speaking, no pillaging—no houses were interfered with that were inhabited—but there is no doubt about it, chickens, pigs and "such like" did suffer some ; and all this on Sunday, December 14th, 1862.

On the 15th the column was moving again. We recrossed the bridge over the Neuse, which we then destroyed, and pushed on towards Whitehall, making a long march of from sixteen to eighteen miles, and coming to a halt late in the evening about three miles from the town. Here, on the morning of the

Skirmish. 16th, a lively skirmish took place, the enemy being posted on the opposite side of the river. For hours the artillery firing was very heavy, and the Rebel sharpshooters annoyed our troops very much. So one hundred sharpshooters were called for from the Twenty-fifth ; ten or twelve went from Company A, and all these men did excellent service. After three or four hours of this fighting, in which the artillery played a conspicuous part, the enemy withdrew, and our troops moved on, coming to a halt a few miles from Goldsboro'. Our troops destroyed a ram that was building at Kinston. The loss to the Union side in this affair was seventy to eighty killed and wounded.

1862.

At night, as we sat around the bivouac fire talking over the events of the day, our sharpshooters began to come in. We had been talking about them; some had been wounded, and one—Moses P. Brown—was reported killed. This Brown was a happy-go-lucky sort of chap, good-natured, great for foraging; and every one seemed sorry that he was killed. "He was not so bad a fellow after all," said one. "That's so," said another, "good-hearted boy," and so on. Just at that moment who should appear but Brown himself, loaded as usual with plunder, which he threw down at our feet with his cheery "Hello, fellers." We were astonished. "Well, I'll be blowed," said one, "if here ain't that *cussed* Brown." How soldier-like—praising him when we thought him dead, cursing him when we found he was alive.

Brown dead and Brown living.

Brown was indeed well loaded down with (of course) eatables. A ham stuck on his bayonet, a pair of chickens, and a bag of sweet potatoes, were the principal things.

1862.

Dec. 17.
Battle of
Goldsboro'

On the morning of the 17th our brigade (Col. Lee) had the advance, and after a short march through pine forests, we heard the sharp reports of rifles ahead, and knew that the enemy had made another stand. At this time a battery came tearing down the road, passed rapidly through the column on its way to the front, and turning into the fields on the right, crossed a small stream, and took a position on a slight elevation that commanded the meadow in front and the railroad beyond. Behind this railroad stood the Rebel brigades, said to be commanded by Evans and Clingman, with Pettigrew as a support. Our regiment crossed the stream, which was small and shallow, and took a position to the left of the battery, which opened on the enemy and made quick work with them. They were thrown into disorder, and soon were in full retreat. They fell back across the river and again formed, when the battery took another position and we followed, and coming to a halt, laid down on the ground close to and in front of the guns, which opened again on the enemy, sending shell directly over our heads. "Lay low, Twenty-fifth," sung out the battery boys; and I think we did. "Down your colors." The flag held upright, was brought down to the ground as directed. The battery boys behaved splendidly; we could hear the orders given to them, and see how quickly they were obeyed. 'It was like the working of a machine. Meantime regiments had been sent to destroy the railroad; this was a remarkable sight. A regiment formed beside the track, and at the word all lifted at once and rolled the track right over and down the bank. Some built fires of sleepers, and laying rails across piled others on them, thus bending the iron out of shape. A Lieutenant Graham, of the Twenty-third New York Battery, volunteered to burn the railroad bridge, which he did successfully, performing a most perilous feat.

1862.

Battle of Goldsboro'

The enemy had again been forced to retire, and we were ordered to fall back, which we did, crossing the little stream again. As we were to be the rear guard we waited for the column to pass. It was quite late in the afternoon, and we were resting quietly, feeling that our day's work was about done, when we noticed a commotion among the battery boys. The cavalry, too, we could see were uneasy, and appeared to be looking intently to the front. Soon we heard the Rebel yell, apparently in the same meadow from which they had been driven, and knew there was trouble ahead. We saw the

—— battery men move the guns forward. Then a call was made for support, and we were ordered back to the field. The enemy charged on our guns, and the batteries began to speak. It was a sight to see how rapidly they were fired. We crossed the little stream once more, reached the desired position, and laid down in close column by division, almost under the guns of Belger's Battery, which we were to support. In the meantime the Rebels formed in three lines and were making for our guns, but these were taking care of themselves. We could hear the boys at the battery talk coolly with each other. "Here is a shot for the old flag!" they shouted as a gun was fired, and a shell went screaming through the air on its deadly mission, making a great lane through the ranks of the Gray. "Here is one for Uncle Abe!" "Here's one for the Twenty-fifth!" and "Here is one for the devil!" as the guns were fired in rapid succession. No machine could have worked more steadily than did Belger's Battery in the fight at Goldsboro' Bridge.

And now the Twenty-fifth boys began to go wounded to the rear. We were in a bad place; shots from both sides passed over our heads, and we could not fire a gun. Our time had not come—

1862.

Battle of Goldsboro'

it did not come in that battle. Our cavalry had meantime charged over and over again, and against that terrible fire from Belger's and Morrison's batteries no human power could stand, so the Rebels fell back across the meadow and beyond the railroad out of sight, leaving the ground thickly strewn with their dead and wounded.

"We were all lying on the ground, shots flying thickly around us, orders to *lay low*. Col. Pickett, expecting an order to advance his regiment, had mounted a stump, and was carefully looking the ground over in his front to get his bearings. 'Lay low, boys,' he repeated, when a soldier looked up at him with the very pat question, 'Why don't you lay low yourself, Colonel?' We heard no answer to the question, but did hear sundry expressions, as 'Good hit,' 'Pretty well put,' and the like."

Again we fell back, but the little stream we had crossed so many times was now swollen to a broad, deep, swift-running torrent, still rising; but we jumped in and struggled through as best we could, holding rifles and cartridge boxes high to keep them dry. The cavalry and artillery had no trouble in crossing, but many of the infantry boys were washed down stream; some got out and some were lost.

Pickett's bravery.

1862.

Burning forest.

It was now dark and grew cold very fast; we were in a sad plight for our clothes froze on us as we marched. We soon reached the woods; these had been set on fire by the troops ahead of us, but this served a good purpose, for it helped to make us warm. It was a thrilling sight; the flames were roaring on both sides of the road, and ahead it was one mass of fire—a glimpse of hell! The sudden rise of the stream was accounted for by the breaking of a dam, some said by the enemy, others by cannon shot.

We bivouacked long after midnight in a corn field. On the 18th we marched all day with only a halt long enough to cook our coffee. Forest on fire as before. "At night, being unable to sleep, I took a stroll through the silent camp. It was midnight, and the fires were burning low, but still bright enough to throw a faint light over the whole camp and its sleeping soldiers. The long line of guns stacked were plainly to be seen. Around and under their guns were the forms of the battery boys, sleeping quietly as kittens; their horses closely guarded and carefully cared for, were near by. In the distance could be seen the gleam of moving bayonets as sentries paced their beats. Here was a soldier, unable to sleep, having a solitary smoke; another making a cup of coffee. In another place two were smoking, talking over in a low tone the incidents of the march. 'Hallo,' said one, 'what regiment?' 'Twenty-fifth Massachusetts,' I replied. 'Have a sit-down, Sergeant,' and he pulled his blanket along for a seat. Soon we were gossiping away as cosy as could be, talking over the events of the expedition, and anticipating the morrow. 'I say, Bill, haul out those potatoes,—done ain't they?' 'Guess so,' and with his bayonet he poked half a dozen sweet potatoes out of the hot embers. Salt was produced, and with a cup of piping hot coffee and the omnipresent hard-tack, we had a good soldiers' supper, eaten with soldiers' appetite. A half-hour spent thus, and extending them an invitation to return the visit, I bade them good night, and made my way back. It was a calm, still night, and above the quiet stars looked down upon this bivouac of twenty thousand men. It was a scene never to be forgotten."

One night we bivouacked near Wise's Forks, filed into a field on the left of the road, stacked arms, and went for rails for our fires. It was a hard effort to get them, but we succeeded at last, and a

Stroll at midnight.

cheery rail fire covered with tin cups full of coffee was a pleasant sight for cold and tired soldiers. While gathering leaves and hunting for rails a comrade discovered a dead Johnny partly covered with leaves. Soon others were found, and Comrade Mayers—I think it was—reported finding "some Johnnies out in the woods all dead." "What are you fretting about then? All dead you say?" "Yes." "Then they won't trouble us before morning, will they?" They did though, for a detail was made to bury them, and the order had to be obeyed. Thirteen dead Confederates were found at this place; the Third New York Cavalry had been through here, and this was the result in part.

1862.

Dead Rebels.

This march back to New Berne, which we reached Sunday the 21st, was severe. The weather was very cold, and one night the water froze in the canteens under our heads, as we laid with our feet to the rail fire. We were absent from New Berne thirteen days, and the Union loss in killed, wounded and missing was five hundred and seventy-five men.

Severe weather.

"On the return from Goldsboro' rations of whiskey were served out to the men. Corporal Elwell had on this occasion taken a large ration, and was making considerable noise, strutting about and calling himself Provost Marshal of Plymouth. This was a hit at Captain Parkhurst, who was Provost Marshal of Plymouth while we were there. It made some disturbance. Colonel Pickett, who was on horseback, rode up and seeing the state of things, could hardly keep down a laugh; but calling Lieutenant Bessey, said: 'Take the Corporal away, or I shall *have* to see him.' Pickett possessed that happy faculty of not *seeing* too much."

1863.

The new year of 1863 found us at New Berne in old Camp Oliver, and for some weeks we had a quiet time of it. February 8th, one hundred guns were fired from Fort Totten, it being the anniversary of the taking of Roanoke Island.

New Year

The weather was very changeable; warm days and cold, often freezing, nights. This caused much sickness. It is but justice to say that the Twenty-fifth was the crack regiment of the Department, and great crowds came every day to witness the dress parade.

"One Sunday, after inspection, all the sergeants being in their tent, Sergeant McLane said he was going to get a pass to go down town. 'What for, Jemsy? Nothing going on in town to-day,' said Burr. 'Well, fellers, we have been out here a year and a

1863.

half, and I have not been to church; I feel as though I ought to go.' 'Good, Jemsy, that's just the way I feel,' said Sergeant Putnam. Jemsy got his pass and departed. The day went by as Sundays always did; the boys amused themselves with reading, writing, slicking up, etc., and profound quiet reigned in Camp Oliver. After dress parade, when all the sergeants were in their tent, Jemsy returned, his appearance, to say the least, not indicating that he had been to church. 'Well, Jemsy, had a good time?' 'Y-o-u b-e-t I have.' 'Go to church?' asked Burr. 'Y-e-s, I did, and would you believe it, I got down on my knees and I'll be G—d d—d to h—l if I could think of a single prayer!'"

Forgotten prayers.

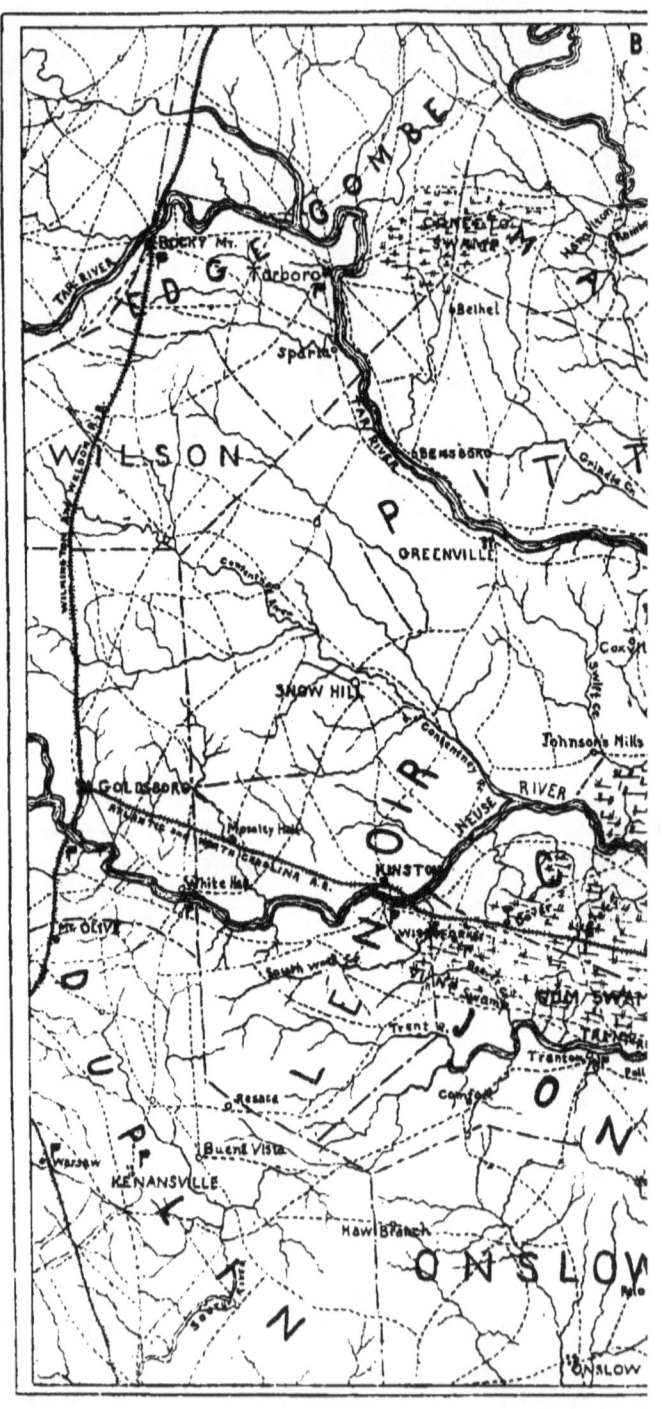

Univ.

CHAPTER IX.

EXPEDITIONS (*Continued*).

ON THE 4th of March Companies A and C went on picket on the Trent road near Deep Gully, joining the companies already there under Captain Denny. The camp was known as Camp Pickett. On the 6th we heard the order while on duty, "Fall in A, fall in. The Twenty-fifth comes." Soon the Regiment made its appearance, and we took our place in line, and started off on another expedition. After a march of a dozen miles towards Kinston, passing the blockade again, we bivouacked in a beautiful spot completely shut in by pine woods and perfectly concealed. This was near the forks of the Trenton and Kinston roads. Companies A, G and K were ordered to be in readiness at midnight to go on a scout, the object being to "gobble up" a body of Rebel infantry on picket five or six miles

1863.

Camp Pickett.

from our bivouac, and to destroy their camp. At the appointed time we left our camp with a company of the Third New York Cavalry in advance. The night was very dark at the start, but we pushed on through woods, swamps and mud towards Kinston for three or four miles, then advancing with more caution as we drew near the picket post of the enemy. Suddenly, crack went a rifle in advance, the cavalry made a dash and the infantry followed at double-quick. This was all very exciting. But that rifle shot would alarm the next post, and we must move on. Soon there was another shot and another dash of the cavalry, in which they succeeded in capturing one of the Rebel pickets; and on we went. A horseman was now heard approaching; the cavalry dismounted and quietly awaited his advance. They challenged and grappled with him; the struggle was fierce but short. No shots fired this time. The horseman is captured and sent to the rear under guard.

As we still pressed on those ahead received the fire of some half-dozen rifles—probably a reserve guard, or the main picket camp. The cavalry had two wounded this time; we had none. An open field was on our left, woods on our right, and open fields beyond. Ahead—perhaps a quarter of a mile —was a dark line of woods, in which was supposed to be the enemy's camp. Skirmishers—Company G, Lieutenant Daly—were thrown out on the right; on the left a portion of Company A, Sergeant Putnam, while the rest of Company A under Lieutenant Bessey, and Company K, Lieutenant Forbes, held the center in the road. The skirmishers of Company A took their place in line in the field as quickly as if it had been broad daylight, and we went forward. A wide, deep ditch was encountered, but with a sort of flying jump the boys managed to cross, and we advanced again. Soon the moon came out from behind the clouds and we could view the whole country in our vicinity. A volley was fired on our right—Company G was catching it. We came to a barn, and geese hissed at us as we passed, but not a gun was fired. It was comical withal, the hissing of those geese, and a low laugh ran down the skirmish line. We approached the woods and still not a shot was fired. A light was seen through the trees, and the forms of tents dimly appeared. We had struck the Rebel camp. We entered the woods, the left of the skirmish line swung around to the right, and we had the camp—a dozen tents—surrounded.

1863.

Attack on the camp.

1863.

The camp taken.

Meantime the troops, with the cavalry in advance, had charged down the road, received a volley from the Rebels, and then driven them. Corporal Jimmy Green ("Spud" we called him) was sent to Captain Denny, who was in command, to report that we had captured the camp, and he ordered it burned. But first we went through it. We found boxes unopened, evidently just received; we opened them with our bayonets and found them filled with good things from home—apples, cake, eggs, etc. We, of course, ate the solids, and—certainly, why not?—drank the fluids, and then proceeded to obey orders. We stirred up the fire, piled on everything that would burn, and soon all was in a blaze.

Bugbee's chickens.

Corporal Bugbee heard chickens cackle. "Kill 'em, boys," he shouted, "Damn 'em, we can eat 'em! Wring their necks!" Very soon there was no more cackling of chickens. But they proved rather expensive to the Corporal, for in his haste to catch them he kicked aside a little roll of paper which was picked up by Comrade White, who found he had sixty dollars in Confederate bills. These, of course, were not passable within our lines, but White exchanged them with North Carolina people for their money, which was current in New Berne, and this he loaned about to the boys, and they, on next pay day, returned it to him in greenbacks! Bugbee got the chickens but lost the money.

1863.

After the camp had been destroyed we made a hasty march back to our bivouac in the woods, reaching there about six o'clock on the morning of the 7th, having marched about a dozen miles since leaving our camp at midnight. We remained here until the next day and then returned to Camp Pickett.

Our boys brought away some things from the Rebel camp,—rifles, knapsacks, and several "Yankee Slayers"*—but nothing of value. Some letters found in the knapsacks which our boys went through, showed a pitiful state of things in the South at that early stage of the war. The following are extracts from a letter which was taken from a knapsack in this camp, and is now in the possession of the writer. It was written by a mother to her sons in the Confederate army.

"*Yankee Slayers.*"

---

*These "Yankee Slayers" were huge, rough blades, one and a half feet long, and quite heavy. They were hammered out by hand, had rude scabbards, and were intended to be hung on the waist-belt. One of these, taken from the Rebel camp, is now in the museum of The Worcester Society of Antiquity. It is, perhaps, unnecessary to say that these terrible-looking weapons were perfectly harmless. I never knew of one of them being used, nor did I ever hear of any person who was injured by one.

1863.

A Southern letter.

febaray the 2ᵈ 1863

Deer Sons   i seet myselfe to Drope you uns a few lins to let you no that i reseved your kind and Welkim leter to nite and i war Mour then gladde to her from you both   these few lins leves us all well at this time . . .   i war glade to her from you uns and sorry to her that you War on picket and had nothing to eat   i want to no Whether you got What litel i sent . .   if you stay thar and if you Dont get kill ner takin prisner i will try and git some boddy to fetch you somthing to eat   time is hard her . . .   i have bin tring to git Wheat and corn ever sins and i cant gite a bite at no prise   corn is Worth from 2 to 3 Dolers and cant git hit at that   they War a Man at town the outher Day and he oferd A hunderd Dolers A barle and cold not git hit at that   Meet they is ofern A Doler and fifty cents A pond and i Dont no What the pepel Will Dow her let lone the pour Solger and hit is harde on both sids . . .

fer What i can under stand you boys is giting [*illegible*] Wicked takin up the pour yankes and taken tha clothing of and pull ther eys opin an ther Moth and standin them up and cusen them and i Want to no Whether hit is so or not   i Dont no Whether hit is so [or] not   i hope hit aint so and i never Want to her of the like beeing Don in ther compny A gane   When i hirde hite hit Made the hare rise one My hed   how Wod i fel to her of your A beeing kill and the yankeys servin you so . . .

the young girls is Wating fer you solgers to come   they say to the olde Men When they come A bout them goe Way you is no solges goe to the War . . .

This expedition was a bold thing to undertake, and was well planned and well carried out. It was only partially successful, however, for the purpose was to capture the entire detachment, whereas we secured only half a dozen prisoners; but we broke up the post and destroyed the camp.

1863.

The troops left for New Berne, Company A remaining at Camp Pickett. On the 13th of March the enemy made a bold attempt to capture New Berne. They approached the town from every available point, driving in our pickets at Deep Gully, and four companies, A, C, G and K, were ordered there. This Deep Gully was a ravine extending from the Trent river some miles towards the Neuse, and having a deep stream of water running through it, not easily crossed except at one place where was a bridge and one or two fords. At the Gully was an earth-work which protected the bridge, and one old *Quaker* gun made it look quite formidable. As the enemy approached near, Company A under Lieutenant Bessey; Company C, Lieutenant Davis; and Company G, Captain Wagely, formed in the rear of the earthwork, Company A at the left. Soon the enemy opened on us with grape shot, which passed harmlessly over our heads as we lay on the ground and crashed into the woods at our rear. Sergeant Wesson ("Old Rats" the boys called him) seeing a large stump directly in his front, ten or twelve feet distant, crawled to it, and feeling quite

Attack at Deep Gully.

secure behind it, looked back to us, and with a motion of his fingers to his nose said, "Don't you wish you were here?" In less than a minute a solid shot struck the stump, which proved to be rotten, and the pieces flew in every direction. Wesson was not injured, and a hearty laugh greeted him as he wriggled back to his place in line.

The place got too warm for us, and we were ordered to fall back, which we did without harm. The cavalry had one man killed. We formed in line of battle with the cavalry on our left, and waited for an attack; hours passed with little firing and no harm done. At the first appearance of the enemy a messenger had been sent to New Berne for help, and about 6 P. M., the balance of the old Twenty-fifth, with the Fifth and Forty-sixth Massachusetts regiments, and part of Belger's Battery, reached us. Our regiment was the first to arrive, and we were glad to see our comrades, and now felt as if we could drive the enemy, although it was reported that they had over a dozen pieces of artillery, some cavalry, and eight or ten regiments.

The enemy were delayed in crossing at the Gully a little while, as our people had destroyed the bridge. Trees had also been felled across the road which added to the delay, but after a time they got into position, and there was considerable firing until dark. That night was freezing cold, and as no fires were allowed we were in a wretched plight. It did seem as though the cold would penetrate to our very bones.

1863.

The next day, the 14th, we were relieved by the Forty-third Massachusetts, and we returned to Camp Oliver, passing on the way our picket camp, and taking our knapsacks with us.

It seems that the attack on New Berne was a failure in every quarter. The gunboats took a hand in it on the Neuse river, and altogether there was quite a lively time. The Rebs at the Gully were under command of General B. B. Hill, while Pettigrew commanded across the Neuse river, opposite New Berne.*

The attack a failure.

There were probably at this time in New Berne, twenty-five thousand men, and an imposing sight was the grand review by General Foster. It was, I think, the largest body of soldiers we ever had in North Carolina.

Grand review.

As one hundred guns were fired on February 8th

* For a full description of this attack on New Berne, see Denny's *Wearing the Blue.*

1863.

in honor of the Battle of Roanoke, so we were to have a holiday on March 14th, in honor of the capture of New Berne; but to accomodate the Rebels in their desire to attack the place on that day, our celebration was put off until the 17th. On the morning of that day crowds gathered on the parade ground to witness the sports. General Foster and staff, also General Palmer, were present, and appeared to enjoy the fun as sensible men should. A boxing match between Captain Tom O'Neil and his brother Jim, was one of the exercises of the day. Sack races followed, in which Company A was represented by Comrade Sawyer, who carried away the prize. Climbing the greased pole caused a deal of merriment. Half a dozen men blindfolded, wheeling wheelbarrows at a mark, were a comical feature in the programme, and chasing greased pigs made much commotion all over the camp, while other sports occupied the time until the middle of the afternoon, when the affair broke up, and the crowds dispersed.

Holiday sports.

Two days after, on the 19th, tents were struck, and the Regiment was on its way to Plymouth on board the steamer *Escort*. As there was not room for the whole regiment on the vessel Companies A,

E and H marched to the barracks used by the Forty-fourth, and remained until the 23d, when the same steamer took the three companies and landed them at Plymouth on the 25th. One night, during our stay at the barracks, we thought it would be—as Comrade Bolster expressed it—*conducive*, if we could have a dance. Leave was obtained to remain up after taps, two fiddles were found in a neighboring regiment, candles procured and the old barracks lighted up, and at it the boys went. But to dance without ladies was a difficulty not reckoned on, and it was, I think, the genius of Private Bolster that overcame it. "Take your caps, fellers; visors to the front, men; visors to the rear, women." 'Tis done, and funny enough, all visors are to the rear! All want to be women. This was soon arranged and the fun began. Mr. (Capt.) Thomas O'Neil and Miss (Lieut.) Daly were the stars of the evening, keeping the crowd in a roar of laughter. For two hours the frolic went on, when orders came "Lights out," and the day ended. This is a trifling incident to note, but there are many such trifling incidents in the every-day life of the soldier. Even in war time, soldiers are not always fighting, nor always on the march; but soldiers are *always* busy,

1863.

Our dance.

—— and if duty does not call them, fun comes to the front.

1863.

A transport ship with six or eight hundred men on board is not the most comfortable place in the world, one great trouble being the lack of facilities for cooking for the multitude. Any soldier will appreciate the situation. The ordinary ship cooking apparatus is at best limited in its capacity, and of no great account with such a crowd. Now the steamer *Escort* was provided with huge boilers in which could be cooked a barrel of beef and a barrel of coffee at the same time; this to us was a godsend and of the greatest benefit to the soldiers.

Ship discomforts.

Since our last visit to Plymouth the town had changed for the worse. It had been occupied by both Union and Confederate troops, and a few weeks before was set on fire by the enemy, and the business portion in the center of the town entirely destroyed. Several large private houses, with elm trees in front, from whose branches hung in long festoons the "Ivy green," were also consumed. But this is war. Our camp was pitched in the burnt district, and in honor of the commander of the gunboat *Commodore Perry*, was named Camp Flusser, Colonel Pickett taking command of the post, and Lieutenant-Colonel Moulton, of the Twenty-fifth Regiment.

Effects of war.

On our arrival at Plymouth Companies A, G and K were highly complimented for their conduct at the Gully on the 13th, and they deserved it. The troops went to work at once on the fortifications just laid out for the defence of the town. A heavy detail was made from each company to work on the fort, besides the regular camp and picket duty; and the pioneers went out daily to clear away the forest and get a good range for the guns. The pioneers often cut down trees four feet through, straight as arrows, and more than one hundred feet high.

1863.

Plymouth again.

Fortifications.

Refugees kept coming down the river, some from a distance of fifty miles, in their dugouts. Some of these boats were quite large; one, I remember, contained three men, three women and six children, with all their household effects. Most of these people were going to New Berne, having been driven from their homes on account of their Union sentiments.

Refugees.

As early as the middle of February we had found wild flowers in bloom in New Berne—violets, myrtle, trailing arbutus and others; and here, at Plymouth, they were very abundant.

Wild flowers.

We had now been over five months without pay, and there was considerable growling; but unless to send it home, which many of us did, it was not of much account, really, for a soldier actually needs little money for himself; still it was "convenient to have in the house," and we were paid shortly after, which made the boys happy for a while.

1863.

Our Camp Flusser was neatly laid out, and the company tents were very comfortable. From the burnt district we got boards for floors, raised our Sibley tents about three feet, putting a sort of curtain of canvas around at the bottom; this made the tents more roomy and very pleasant. But this was not all. We stole, or rather, *found*, doors, which with a little rough carpenter work we put in place in our tents. These doors had knobs, and the whole thing worked admirably. We did not get any door-bells for our tents, as it was thought we could get along without them; but think of it—soldiers without door-bells to their tents!

Camp Flusser.

No door-bells.

We picked up while at Plymouth, as soldiers will, many pets—a curious lot—squirrels, owls, raccoons, birds, and little darkies, the latter quite useful in blacking shoes and such odd jobs. The habit of dipping snuff in the South has been spoken of. One day a little white girl passed by the camp, and a soldier, observing a stick protruding from her

Pets.

mouth, asked, "What have you in your mouth little girl?" "My snuff stick," was the reply. "What, do you chew tobacco?" "Oh, no; I dont chew, I dip." "How old are you?" "I'm seven," was the reply. What a sight was that.

1863. A youthful "dipper."

An effort was made while at Plymouth to get up another dance, and in looking about for a place a little brick church was selected. In the first place it was quite central, and then it was large enough; so the church door was opened—whether with or without a key I do not remember—space was cleared of seats on the floor, candles obtained, fiddlers found, and all promised well. Meantime a little incident was transpiring not calculated on by the getters-up of the scheme. A squad of soldiers had discovered at no great distance from our camp, a small house, in which was found that cheerful-looking carriage, the village hearse. This was run out of the building; it had a covered top and open sides, and a singular idea popped into the head of one of our boys. "I say fellers, suppose we run this team around town and pick up the boys and take them to the dance." There were no horses, so two or three soldiers got hold of each thill, and "she is all right," One mounts to the driver's seat, and one

Frolic with the hearse.

1863.

Pickett after the boys.

—— crawls inside, smoking his pipe, saying, "I'll be the first passenger." It was comical enough—a soldier stretched at full length, and smoke rolling out in puffs from the inside of that dismal-looking vehicle, all ready for a start. But suddenly a soldier puts in an appearance with "Look out boys, Colonel Pickett has ordered the arrest of every man engaged in this church dance business. Take care of yourselves"; and he took care of himself by disappearing around the corner. What a change was there. The driver got down from his seat, and the passenger slid out, making, as one expressed it, quicker time than was usual with passengers in that carriage, the hearse was taken back into the house, doors shut with a hurried slam, and the boys disappeared to take care of themselves. It proved as was said, that Pickett had ordered the arrest of all concerned. The lights were put out and the church closed; quite a number of the men were arrested, and—Plymouth was saved. The upshot of the matter was a severe reprimand to those in custody—and that was enough. The affair made some talk for a day or two, and Comrade Bolster proposed that, as there had been so much fuss about it, we should pick up the little d—d church, and send it home as a *momentum* of the occasion. This expression brought down the house—Bolster generally did when he spoke.

1863.

We found in Plymouth hand cards made at Leicester, Massachusetts, by Whittemore; and it is a little singular that they were found by Leicester boys.

While we were at Plymouth, Washington, North Carolina, was surrounded by the Rebels, who laid siege to the place with twelve thousand men. General Foster was there with only twelve hundred men, but he held the place. A steamer with ammunition and a few troops run the blockade, and relieved the hard-worked garrison; and General Foster run the gauntlet one night on the steamer *Escort*, with the loss of one or two men, and reached New Berne in safety, intending to return at once and relieve the place. This was not necessary, however, for the enemy had got enough of it, and one night raised the siege and vanished, leaving Washington and the Tar river free. This defence of Washington, though little talked about and little known, was a brilliant affair, and reflected great credit upon General Foster, and spoke well for the pluck and endurance of the men under his command.

Siege of Washington.

1863.

On the 3d of May we were relieved by Wessel's Brigade, and at seven P. M., left Plymouth on the steamer *Thomas Collyer*, Commander Flusser and his sailors giving us a display of fireworks with hearty cheers as we left the old town. We reached New Berne on the afternoon of the 4th, after a delightful sail; and on the 5th of May had our tents pitched once more in old Camp Oliver.

Bone carving.
As at Roanoke Island the boys had the fever for making briar wood pipes, so at New Berne the rage for bone-work prevailed to an alarming extent during the remainder of our stay at Camp Oliver. Comrade Henry Goulding was the most expert at this business, and turned out some really very fine work in the shape of rings, crosses, scarf-pins, etc., all beautifully carved. This fever for bone cutting pervaded the whole Regiment, and it served to while away many an hour of dull camp life.

Furloughs
We had now been in the service of Uncle Sam over a year and a half, and in accordance with orders received, we were having furloughs of thirty days granted us, a certain number from each company of the Regiment going, and on their return another lot departing, and so on. This was very pleasant, and was encouraging to the soldiers. Every man

who returned from furlough would be surrounded by a crowd of soldiers eager to catch every word he uttered as he told the story of what he had seen at home.

1863.

At midnight of May 21st we were on the march again, this time in the direction of Bachellor's Creek. We had been on the road about two hours, and the men were plodding along tired and sleepy, when an unusual noise was heard at the head of the column, and the men of the companies before us dropped out to the right and left of the road as though a squad of cavalry was charging down the line. Company A did the same and those in our rear followed suit; and in a moment, as it were, the road was clear of soldiers; scarcely one man could be seen standing in it. In their precipitation the men fell helter-skelter over one another, and as they picked themselves up and got back to their places in the road again, the question was asked by every one: "What was that?" and the answer, "What was it?" Some declared they saw the form of a horse pass like a flash down the center of the road; others thought it was a deer that had got frightened and dashed into the line; and others saw nothing, but all got out of the way. The question "What was

Another march.

What was it?

it?" has never been satisfactorily answered. After the march was resumed, the men talked the affair over, and all declared they would not get out of the way again if the devil himself should come.

We had not been half an hour on the road, and the men were getting drowsy again, when a noise similar to the first reached our ears from somewhere in advance, and a few soldiers were dropping out of the road again from the companies ahead, and about as quickly as before. But Company A must have the credit of remaining in line this time. "We brought our rifles to the 'Charge bayonets' and waited for—nothing." It was really nothing this time, and the affair created a great deal of mirth as we proceeded on our way.

At early daylight we came to a halt near the railroad leading to Goldsboro'. In the middle of the afternoon we got on board a train of cars and moved some five or six miles towards Goldsboro', and joining the Fifth and Twenty-seventh Massachusetts Regiments, marched to Core Creek and bivouacked till midnight. The march was then resumed, the Twenty-fifth having the advance after crossing Core Creek. Company K, Captain Denny, was thrown out as advance guard, and we moved on quickly but quietly, with no signs of an enemy until about 4 A. M., when the advance run on to the Rebel pickets and drove them in. The Regiment now filed into a field on the right, and formed in line of battle. Companies K (Captain Denny) and E (Captain O'Neil) were sent out as skirmishers, and soon discovered a long line of earthworks, and both parties commenced firing. This continued two hours or more, when we heard loud cheering and volleys of musketry in the enemy's rear, and we knew our boys, under Colonel Jones, of the Fifty-eighth Pennsylvania, were charging. Company A, Captain Goodwin, was now sent to join the skirmish line, which was advancing at double-quick; the line of defence was soon reached, and Company A swarmed over the earthworks like bees; and being attacked both in front and in the rear, the Johnnies were at a disadvantage. They scattered in every direction; we took one hundred and sixty-five prisoners, and proceeded to destroy the works as best we could. We held the position, which was a strong one, until 5 P. M., when the object of the expedition being accomplished, and as the enemy, having been strongly re-enforced, were coming down the railroad, we commenced a retreat to Core Creek.

1863.

Engagement with the enemy.

Co. A first in the earthworks.

1863.

The retreat.

In Gum Swamp.

The Twenty-fifth Regiment, with a company of cavalry, and one piece of artillery, acted as rear guard, the enemy following close on our heels, shelling us but doing no harm. We reached Core Creek about 10 P. M., and bivouacked for the night. On the 23d we moved early in the direction of the railroad, intending to take the train at Bachellor's Creek; but a heavy force of the enemy was found posted on the railroad in our front, at the point where the road we were traveling crossed it, and we were fired upon from our right, and in our rear they were close upon us. We were getting into a bad place, but our artillery with some trouble dispersed our opposers, and we passed on. The enemy were, no doubt, trying to cut us off; to avoid this we made quite a detour through what is, properly speaking, Dover Swamp, but was then called "Gum Swamp"; and by this name it will be always known to the members of the Twenty-fifth Regiment. On leaving the road we plunged at once into this swamp. It was more than knee-deep with mud and water, its bushes and brambles were interlaced with vines, and it was with the greatest difficulty that we could cut our way along. As hour after hour passed it seemed as if there was no end to it. Not a breath of air was stirring, and the sun poured down an intense heat upon us. The boys began to give out. The great cry was: "Water, water." We tried to strain the swamp water through our handkerchiefs, but it was horrible and we could not drink it. Fainting, panting for breath, struggling along, men dropped down where they stood, and it seemed impossible to get them any further. And yet, there was a sort of grim humor through it all; the old jokes would occasionally come to the surface: "Why did we go for sogers," said one. "Give it up," was the reply. "Because we were foolish cusses," said another. But no song enlivened this dreadful march through Gum Swamp; it took all the strength, all the pluck the men possessed to stagger along and keep their failing spirits up. Comrade Forbes, who had been detailed for hospital service, and had done little or no duty with the Company, was with us in the swamp, with a large box of medicines, etc., on his back. Doctor Rice, the Regimental Surgeon, was also here; and, of course, all were on foot, and one man was as good as another. "I say, Forbes, you don't carry a rifle, but you have to carry the Doctor's pill box." "Yes, and I'd tote it to hell if only Old Rice had to go 'long afoot!" "Billy," said

1863.

In Gum Swamp.

1863.
—— another (to Billy Lyon), "don't you wish you was home?" "Bah! home is a fool to this place."

But all this ceased after a while, and no sound was heard save the splashing of the mud and water as we pushed slowly on. After some four hours of this dreadful marching, the cry ran along the line: "The railroad! the railroad!" This was good news, indeed, and with desperate efforts we struggled on, *Through the swamp* and were soon at the railroad, where we scrambled on to the freight cars awaiting us, and like starving men ate the rations that were soon brought. We reached New Berne at 5 P. M., Saturday, May 23d, and were at home in Camp Oliver.

We marched thirty miles on this expedition. Several men had to be brought out of the swamp on stretchers, and it was said that two or three died before they could be got out. At dark of this day the Rebs, who had followed us, attacked our force at Bachellor's Creek. This post was gallantly defended, but Colonel Jones—he who was in command on this expedition—was shot dead.

In June of 1863 the troops were employed in building fortifications, and as the thermometer would often show over one hundred in the shade, work ceased during the hottest part of the day. This labor in such extremely hot weather was very trying to the men, and the sick list was soon doubled. The daily drills were kept up, and the Twenty-fifth was never allowed to play second fiddle in that respect.

1863.

On the 4th of July the Company was ordered to the breastworks near Fort Totten. A cavalry expedition had started from New Berne, and the infantry were to stay in the fortifications until it returned, which it did on the 7th, and the Company marched back to Camp Oliver. On the 17th of July the Company went on another expedition. Crossing the Neuse river and landing at Fort Anderson, we marched at once into the country. The weather was intensely hot and the roads heavy with sand, making the marching very hard. We halted at an old, weather-beaten church, and from its pulpit Comrade Daniel T. Eaton gave us a spicy temperance lecture. Meantime the cavalry passed us on a raid towards Tarboro'. They had with them very inoffensive looking machines with which to destroy railroads. They could with ease, they said, turn a red-hot rail into a cork-screw with them.

On the move.

Beyond some sharp skirmishing with the enemy nothing was done by the infantry. On our return

1863.

A hard march.

march water gave out. Our canteens were *squeezed* dry, and with parched lips and swollen tongues, we dragged along to Fort Anderson; but before we reached it many fell down into the hot sand from sheer exhaustion as we marched, and with difficulty were made to move on. As we approached the fort the boys there saw us and took in the situation at a glance. They had pails of water ready for us, into which we thrust our faces as dogs do into a running stream. The Nectar of the Gods was—cold water! After a short rest at the fort we recrossed the Neuse and were home again, July 20. Distance marched, thirty miles.

After a few days' rest (camp duties performed and drill kept up), on July 25th we were once more away, four companies, A, E, G and H going on board the steamer *Rucker*, and landing Sunday, P. M., at Winton, on the Chowan river. We bivouacked on the banks of the stream, and shortly after the cavalry arrived and started off on an expedition to *Scouting.* Weldon. The next day Companies A and E under Captain Tom O'Neil, started off on a scout to Coleraine, and succeeded in capturing forty horses, ten bales of cotton, six hundred pounds of tobacco, and any number of mules and carriages, while negroes by hundreds followed us on our return march to Winton, with little bundles tied up and swung on sticks over their shoulders, shouting "We's gwine to liberty, hi-yah, gwine to liberty!" The negroes would stop work in the fields, gaze at the Yankee column a few minutes, drop hoe or axe, and fling up their old hats and shout "Gwine to liberty!" Their day had come at last. At some plantations the mistress of the house would try to stop the slaves from leaving, but it was of no use. "Missis, we's agwine to liberty." On all the plantations no white men were visible—the darkies said "all in de Rebel army." A motley procession it was as we reached our bivouac at Winton. We had been thirty-five hours absent, and had marched thirty miles in twenty-four hours, actual marching time.

"Gwine to liberty"

The next day, Companies G and H, under Captain Harrington, started on a similar scout. They were gone twenty-four hours, and brought in twelve bales of cotton, twenty horses and mules with harnesses, etc., and a large quantity of tobacco. July 31st we went on board transports again, and reached New Berne on the 1st of August.

The month of August proved a sickly one for the Company. At times over twenty men would assemble at surgeon's call, and on one occasion at roll call, only sixteen men answered to their names for duty. At one time Companies A and E were in Camp Oliver alone, part of the Regiment being in Washington, N. C., some on picket, some in hospitals and some on furlough. Early in September the Company was put on picket again at the Red House. This old place looked like many a New England farm-house. Surrounded by woods, and with white tents on each side, it formed a pretty picture. We had for neighbors the One-hundred-and-thirty-first New York. This regiment had one company of (said to be) half-breed Indians; they proved to be good scouts but poor soldiers. Among the pets at this camp was a huge brown bear.

One Sunday it was announced that our Parson would pay us a visit with his lady Sunday school teachers; and it was expected that we would be in condition to receive them. Everything was put in order, quarters nicely cleaned up, and the men looked very neat and trim. Corporal Bugbee, acting as provost, whose duty it was to keep the grounds clean, was attending to this as the wagon containing the delegation hove in sight, and he drew off his men, intending to complete the job later, while the vehicle came up, and its precious freight entered the Red House. Hours passed; the soldiers waited patiently in their quarters, but no visitors appeared. Meanwhile a merry time they had in the house—judging from the peals of laughter frequently heard. "Guess they're praying, ain't they?" said one. "I reckon," said another. Corporal Bugbee in the afternoon started again to finish his work of cleaning up the grounds, and was busy with three or four men when the wagon was brought up to take the party back to New Berne. As the ladies stepped into the wagon one exclaimed, "Why, we have forgotten the tracts!" "So we have," said another; and a bundle of tracts was thrown out on the ground "without note or comment." Corporal Bugbee quietly called one of his men, and said, pointing to the bundle, "Remove that to the rubbish heap!" The soldier with his shovel scooped up the sanctified package, and "without note or comment," tossed it on to the dirt heap. The ladies looked at one another with astonishment depicted upon their fine faces, and drove off amid such exclamations as "Did you ever," etc. We never saw our Parson or his teachers at any of our picket camps again. The men who witnessed this little incident enjoyed it

1863.

Incident of the tracts.

much; and by the twinkle of his eye it was plain to see that the Corporal appreciated the humor of the act.

While on duty at the Red House we had abundance of fruit, especially grapes. Just outside or beyond our outpost, at what was called the Shute place, was a grape-vine, on which hung—so the boys reported—bushels of excellent grapes; and judging from the grapes brought to camp from this vine, they were correct. So one morning the new picket guard going to relieve those on duty, took for each man two extra haversacks, and on reaching the outpost a squad was made up to visit the Shute place. The plantation was deserted and the house had been destroyed, but the grape-vine was there; and we saw at once that the stories told by the boys had not been exaggerated. The vine was of enormous size, growing over a trellis six or eight feet from the ground, and covered a space—to guess at it—of ten to fifteen feet wide and fifty or sixty feet long. It was loaded down with the finest Scuppernongs. We posted our guard, and in a very short time had every haversack full besides our jackets, and jogged back towards our camp at the Red House. It was said that over forty bushels of grapes had been picked from this vine in one season. The darkies told us: "Better not eat dose grapes. Gib you de chills." "Bah!" said a soldier, "we'll eat the grapes and d—n the chills!" We did eat them, and we thought them healthy. The grapes actually seemed to cure those who had the chills.

The people in New Berne said they tried to avoid the early morning air on account of the chills; also the heat of the day and the night air, for the same reason. It may be that they were right, but we soldiers had to take it all in. Morning or night air or heat of the day—it was all the same to us; and though nearly all of us had chills, yet we surely did not have them worse or more frequently than the residents of New Berne.

On one of the plantations in this neighborhood we found a girl fifteen years old, who said she had never been to New Berne, only eleven miles distant, and was hardly ever off the old plantation, yet was never lonesome. Talk about a quiet life!

Life on picket at the Red House passed rapidly away. We were not often disturbed while there, though on October 22d, Dr. Rice and his orderly, Private Savage of Company A, were captured while riding from Red House to another picket camp in

1863.

Chills.

Dr. Rice captured.

1863.

broad daylight. Dr. Rice was exchanged the next month, but Savage died a prisoner at Richmond. One night we were turned out twice by shots fired in the woods near by, but we had no serious trouble while here. We had now been two years in the service of the United States.

The month previous (September) Colonel Pickett assumed command of the sub-district of the Pamlico, from which he was relieved the following December.

Night march.

On the night of the 24th of October, about 9 o'clock, we left the Red House in heavy marching order, and proceeded to New Berne, about eleven miles. By some mistake, it was said, wagons went to New Berne nearly empty, while the soldiers marched heavily loaded over the same road. We reached New Berne at 3 A. M. of the 25th, and secured a couple of hours' sleep in and around our old cook house, the only building on the ground besides the guard house. The old camp ground looked deserted and dreary enough, not a tent standing where so many had stood in months past; and the place that had been our home so long was desolate indeed, At 5 P. M. of the same day we got on board a train of freight cars, and started for Beaufort, bidding good-bye forever to old Camp Oliver.

Camp Oliver had been in existence about sixteen months, and during a great portion of this time it had been occupied by some part of the Twenty-fifth Regiment; and the boys had come to speak of it as *home*.

1863.

It commenced to rain soon after leaving New Berne, and the train sped on through the mist and darkness, the boys feeling sober and wondering what would come next. Reaching Beaufort (or rather, Morehead City) we went on board our old steamboat, the *S. R. Spaulding*, which was crowded to its utmost. We made an attempt to put to sea, but were unable to get around Cape Lookout on account of heavy weather; so we anchored under the lee of the Cape, close to the lighthouse, for the night. Next morning (October 27th) we succeeded in doubling the Cape, and pushed on around Cape Hatteras (the fourth time for many of us) with fortunately a comparatively calm sea; and still on between Capes Charles and Henry, entering Chesapeake Bay. We went past Fortress Monroe where our fleet had its rendezvous when we started on the Burnside expedition, nearly two years before; and at length reached Newport News at the mouth of the James river; and on the 2d of November Camp

At sea.

1863.

Upton was formed, named after our old Colonel. At this camp Dr. Rice returned to the Regiment, having been exchanged.

When we first landed at Newport News we had shelter tents given out to us. These were strips of light canvas five or six feet square, with buttons and button-holes around the edges. Two of these buttoned together and drawn over a support something like an A tent, formed a shelter under which two men could crawl like dogs, their rubber blankets keeping them from the ground. A tents were given us later, and the place began to look more like a camp. As in New Berne we had raised the Sibley tents and added a curtain of canvas, so here we built a kind of stockade of pine slats—a narrow, rough sort of clapboard, six to eight inches wide and four feet long—and mounted the A tent on top. This made a roomy place, but we had to stop the cracks with mud "to keep the wind away." These slats were cut from pine logs by the darkies, who charged us one dollar per hundred for those four feet long and a dollar and a quarter for the six feet lengths. We had boys detailed to cut these slats, and after a little practice some cut them as readily as the darkies.

Camp Upton.

In the early part of December Colonel Pickett

returned to the Regiment and assumed command. While here at Newport News we had stoves introduced into some of the tents. They were tunnel-shaped, made of sheet iron, and had no bottom; and were placed on the ground, the pipe going up through the top of the tent. They worked very well. In the Sergeants' tent we had a little coal stove that had followed us from North Carolina; and Sergeant Wesson ("Rats") had found some hard coal in an old cellar-hole where a building had been burnt close by, so with a coal fire we were kept very comfortable. At first it would smoke in spite of all we could do. Wesson tried everything he could think of to stop it, but to no purpose. We cut off an old boot leg and fitted it on to the top of the pipe; that worked well for a while, but the heat destroyed it. It was evident our pipe was not long enough—"That's what's the matter." We went outside to reconnoiter. Our neighbors' (next company's) tent backed up to ours. Their stove did not smoke and their pipe was one section higher than ours. Rats put his fore finger to his nose and looked very wise, got a cracker box, placed it close to our neighbors' tent, mounted it, and with leather gloves quietly and quickly removed the upper section from

1863.

A smoky stove.

—— their pipe and placed it on our own. We retired to our tent and seated ourselves on our bunks to "wait the turn of events." Presently from our neighbors' tent: "Hallo, Company A Sergeants; how does your stove work?" "First-rate, real comfortable; how does yours go?" "It smokes like thunder!" They went out of their tent and we heard them discussing the state of affairs; we slipped out and listened to their story, and when it was told Rats quietly remarked, "Your pipe ain't long enough, that's what's the matter." "I vow, I thought our pipe *was* longer than that." "It looks short compared with ours," said Wesson, "you get another length of pipe and you'll be all right." We retired to our tent again, and soon we hear from the other: "Well, I don't understand this." "I do," said Rats in a low tone; and he evidently did. Our stove did not smoke any more but—Rats did.

1863.

Rats' practical joke.

One day a comrade reported: "Sergeant, I've found a lot of bricks out here in the weeds (which were quite high all around the camp); detail a squad of men to go and get 'em, and we'll have an *oven* and *baked beans* tomorrow morning." The detail was made; and soon eight or ten Company A boys were seen coming through the weeds, each

Our oven.

loaded down with bricks; and in a short time an oven was built, and we did have baked beans for breakfast the next morning, to the astonishment of our neighbors, who said, "That's it; Company A always has the best of everything." Very true; we did, but we got it ourselves.

1863.

In plain sight at low tide, and but a few rods from shore, were the wrecks of the frigates *Congress* and *Cumberland* sunk by the Rebel ram *Merrimack;* also the two-turreted monitor *Roanoke*, and later the captured Rebel ironclad *Atlanta*.

Wrecks.

At a review early in December General Foster bade his old soldiers farewell, in consequence of his transfer to another department; and Major-General Benjamin F. Butler assumed command. General Heckman, formerly Colonel of the Ninth New Jersey, took command of our brigade, which was known as "Heckman's Flying Brigade," sometimes spoken of as the "Red Star Brigade," from the flag at headquarters. It was a severe blow to the old North Carolina soldiers to lose General Foster, but he had the good wishes of every man of his old command. While at this camp sickness thinned our ranks to a great extent, and Company A on occasions turned out but twenty-three men for duty.

Gen. B.F. Butler.

CHAPTER X.

CAMP, MARCH, AND BIVOUAC.

WE HAVE now followed Company A from the muster-in at Camp Lincoln to Camp Upton in Virginia. We have seen the Company in camp, in battle, on the march, and in bivouac; we have seen how the men behaved under the most trying circumstances. Let us now leave them for a while in comfortable quarters at Camp Upton, and look a little closer into the daily life of the soldier in active service. Every veteran has had, scores of times, questions asked him which show little knowledge of soldier life on the part of the inquirer, and which seem to one familiar with it hardly worth answering; but comrades must remember that our children, as well as the great mass of the people, know as little of these things as we ourselves did at the start; and it may be well to satisfy their inquiries, often ex-

Ignorance of soldier life.

pressed, as, How do soldiers prepare for an expedition? How do they march, sleep and eat, build fires in stormy weather? etc. In attempting to answer, the simplest way, perhaps, will be to describe soldier life in camp and bivouac, and on a march.

When we speak of a camp, the idea suggests itself at once of a soldier's home, to a certain extent permanent; while bivouac is at the most but a temporary halt or rest. In camp we expect to find comfortable tents pitched in regular order, company streets formed, good quarters for cook houses, grounds in perfect order for parades and the like; while in bivouac no tents are pitched, and none are carried on marches in war time. In active service on a march there is no time to fool away pitching tents, and we expect, at most, only a few hours' rest. It may be—and usually is—for the night, but all are ready to move at a minute's notice. In camp the soldier gradually gathers all sorts of conveniences around him; in his tent we often find board floors, stools and benches made of cracker boxes, and very comfortable bunks to sleep in. In bivouac all these are done away with; the soldier sleeps on the ground rolled in his blanket, as best he can. He cooks his coffee in bivouac—every man for him-

Camp vs. bivouac.

self—while in camp the company cooks attend to all that.

In a wet, swampy country bivouacking is wretched business; but on any dry ground it is certainly superior to tenting, and is the healthier of the two. The A tents, which held six men with all their equipments, were close, stifling things at best; the Sibley tents were much superior, being higher and more airy.

Preparations for a march. In starting from camp on a march—say at 4 A. M.—the company cooks are ordered in advance to have rations ready at the proper time; and they *are* ready, even if it takes all night to do it. The men are roused, and go to the cook house to draw their rations of cooked meat, hard bread, ground coffee, and sugar—perhaps three days' allowance; and (a very important item) the canteen is filled with cold water. The soldiers don their equipments, form in the company street in two ranks, and count off so that each man will know his place in marching by the flank in fours. The company is then marched to the parade ground, where the regimental line is formed. In leaving the camp it is by the flank in fours. No music accompanies the soldiers on these marches, so no attempt is made at keeping step;

but the order "Route step" is given, and the men "go as you please," the fours simply keeping together and marching abreast. The order "Arms at will" follows, and the men carry their rifles in the most comfortable way, at "right shoulder shift" generally; and go jogging along, talking, laughing, telling stories, etc. At the proper time the order "Halt" is heard, and every man is in his place with rifle to the shoulder; "Front," and like a machine the men face to the front, and the regimental line is formed, every man in the same position he was when he started. At a halt every soldier looks out for his own rifle and never loses sight of it; it must be within reach at any time and all the time; but at a bivouac for the night, when safe to do so, guards are posted and the guns are stacked. The men go for water and wood—rails, usually; fires are quickly built, and as quickly covered with tin cups filled with water from the "old canteen" if it contains any, if not, a search is made for some.

The way they march.

The boys are about making coffee. Shall we see how they do it? Fire of fence rails to start with—fence rails make the best possible fire for cooking coffee at a bivouac. Now the tin cup, holding a quart, filled with water, is placed on the fire. Now

—— two or more heaping table-spoonfuls of ground coffee is added (Uncle Sam used to give his boys excellent coffee in the army). Stir gently and watch carefully. See the rich golden color as you keep stirring. Watch the bubbles as they appear and disappear on the surface of this amber-colored sea. Now gently put in sugar as you may desire. Still stirring it begins to boil. Saints and Ministers of Grace! What an aroma is that which greets our expectant nostrils. Odors from Araby the blest— incense to the gods! Steady now—it must not boil too long. Insert your bayonet into the hole in the handle of your cup—a hole you punched there for this very purpose—and lift it with its fragrant, steaming contents from the fire. Now from the old canteen throw in a dash of cold water to settle it, and—it is done. Now for the haversack. Salt horse and hard-tack—usually with something better;* it depends somewhat on the country we have been traveling through—and with a soldier's staving appetite, what a supper is that! Is it the coffee, or appetite, or both?

Coffee making

---

* Sometimes a few onions or a bit of cabbage have been carried for miles in the haversack, and now they work in first-rate. There *is* a place to eat onions and cabbage—around the bivouac fire.

Sometimes a soldier will accidentally hit a rail with his foot, shaking the contents of all the tin cups. What a rumpus follows. "Get out of that" says one. "Can't you pick up your cracker boxes (brogans) easier than that?" says the second. "Look at the cuss, trying to run his gunboats (brogans again) around the camp fire." A shower of such talk greets the ears of the unlucky offender, who for a while keeps quiet, to say the least.

A rumpus

Now it is time to turn in and get some sleep if possible. Let us step out from the glare of the firelight into the darkness, and look at the scene before us. How strongly the features of the men are brought out by the light of the blazing fire. What healthy brown faces they are. In paintings we have such scenes as this, but this is the *living* picture. The fires are burning low, but here and there the smoke is still curling gracefully up in the cool night air; and now, as some one stirs up the smoldering embers and puts on fresh rails, a shower of sparks, like golden bees, floats quietly away as the spray of a fountain in the sunlight. Here is a soldier by himself smoking his pipe, and no doubt thinking of home; there are two fellows—chums—curled up together *spoon-fashion*, with their feet to

A look at the bivouac.

—— the fire, capes of their overcoats drawn over their heads, sleeping as quietly as kittens; others are talking in a low tone of a face they miss to-night— a face they will never see more around the bivouac fire. They gradually become silent, and roll themselves in their blankets and overcoats, and sleep. Thus the men disappear, the fires are left to burn themselves out, and silence reigns over the sleeping bivouac.

How they sleep.
Some sleep on their backs; others sleep on their sides, using cartridge box for pillow; others roll up, three or four together, the last man in tucks up the rest and then wriggles his way into the middle; and all have their rubber blankets to lay on the ground. The old soldier, if left to himself, selects at once the best place to spread his blanket, his first point being protection from rain and wind; and a rubber blanket is admirably adapted for the purpose—all sorts of shelters can be made with it. I do not see how the soldiers could have got along without their "gum blankets," as the Johnnies called them.

In seeking shelter from the wind your old soldier would not select a place under a tree. It is a mistake often made by the inexperienced soldier to choose a spot to spread his blanket under some large tree, with dense foliage above but no protection from the wind below; and this protection from the wind that blows is what he wants. The veteran finds some thick low bushes through which the wind cannot easily penetrate, or rigs up his rubber blanket in some sheltered spot, so that it will serve as a screen or shield. The tree would give him a sort of roof, which is not needed in a clear, windy night. A man sleeping on the ground lies pretty flat and takes up little room, so that any thick shelter that is knee-high is shield enough from any wind that blows, provided the wind cannot blow through it. I have made a good shelter by cutting down bushes and sticking them in the ground thickly together. We used to think when lying on the ground with the enemy's shot and shell flying over us, that we could lie as thin as a plank; some thought as thin as a board; while Comrade Bolster declared that he could lay as thin as a shingle; but when the bullets pierced the very caps on our heads, taking a lock of hair by which to be remembered, we wished we could lie flatter than that.

Shelter at night.

If it be a rainy night it is the roof over his head the soldier wants; and here, again, the rubber

—— blanket comes in play. We have seen how, at New Berne, the soldiers made shelters from the rubber blankets to the best advantage, and it need not be repeated here. The rubber blanket in those days was two yards long, a yard and a quarter wide, and weighed three pounds. It was indeed the soldier's friend. The woolen blanket weighed about five pounds, and measured two and a quarter by one and three quarters yards.

The soldier's friend.

There are more ways than one to prepare a place to sleep on the ground. It is true an old soldier *can* sleep anywhere—on a plank, or on a rock even; but he will not if he can do any better—he will take the best of what there is every time. There is a way to sleep comfortably on dry ground. "I was once spreading my rubber blanket on the ground preparing to turn in, when an old soldier from another regiment, who was passing by, said: 'If you want to sleep well, dig a place for your hips, man.' I looked up, and he continued: 'Scoop out a place for your hips three or four inches deep, and another about half as deep for your shoulders, then spread your rubber and lie in the hollows, and you'll sleep like a top, sir.' I thanked him and followed his advice, and certainly never slept so well on a march

How to sleep.

before." The point seems to be "Make the bed fit your body," not your body fit the bed, as it would have to on any hard surface like a board or hard ground. But this cannot always be done, so the soldier must try other ways. If a fellow is lucky enough to find two logs, he can have a capital place for his blanket between them, and they will keep the wind off.

There are pleasures in bivouac that are entirely lost in camp or tent life. There is no mistake about it, a man breathes better; and it is a pleasure to lie half asleep and listen to the sounds of life around on every side; watch the motions of the men, and hear them talk, joke or sing as they move about the fires, smoking as they always do at such times; and later, to awake when the fires are low, and all sounds of man are hushed, to hear the wind go murmuring by, and watch the stars in a beautiful, clear night; or to catch the lonely cry of some swift-winged night bird as it flies quietly past, or, may be, hear the voice of a wild animal from afar off; and then the sleeper's eyes close dreamily to open no more till the bugle sounds reveille. All this is impossible in tent life.

Pleasures of the bivouac.

But there is a reverse side to this: say a freezing

—— cold night, as on our return march from Goldsboro', when the water froze in the canteens under our heads as we lay on the ground with our feet to the fire; or at other times when we had to walk about all night to keep from being chilled through; or again, cold, stormy nights, with the ground soaked with water, and the rain falling doggedly all night long. These are certainly not pleasant pictures to contemplate; but still, the soldier with a good rubber blanket, a thick, warm woolen one, and a stout overcoat, is pretty well prepared for any sort of weather; and then, there are more pleasant, comfortable nights than stormy ones, more warm ones than cold; and, given, tents crowded to suffocation, or a chance in the open air, I think most soldiers would prefer the latter.

The reverse side.

After all, it is coming pretty near nature, this bivouac life; and men get thoroughly saturated with that spirit of wild freedom that possessed the old freebooters. It is easy to see how soldiers long absent from home, under a beloved and victorious commander, could be led almost anywhere—no expedition would be too hazardous. Witness the legions of Alexander and Hannibal, and the armies of Napoleon.

On marches orders are sometimes issued against —— foraging. This is very good. "Private property to be respected," etc. Quite right. Such orders are always obeyed in a general way; but suppose a soldier *does* pick up a pair of chickens, what then? An instance of this. On a certain march in North Carolina orders had been given that there must be no foraging. We all understood it. One day at a halt late in the afternoon, a soldier came slowly up to the fire, rifle on his shoulder with a ham stuck on his bayonet, and a pair of chickens in one hand. At this moment who should appear but the Colonel himself, riding slowly along the line; and meeting the forager face to face. We expected there would be a scene—and there was. "What did you pay for chickens to-day, my lad?" asked Colonel Pickett. "I didn't pay nothin' for 'em, sir." It was easy to see that the Colonel was anything but angry, but it would not do to show it; so, severely: "You heard the orders against foraging?" "Why yes sir, I did," said the man, standing erect in the position of a soldier, with the chickens still hanging by his side, and the ham sticking on his bayonet; and he expecting to have his head taken off right there. It was too comical a sight; the Colonel could not stand

Foraging.

Caught in the act.

—— it, but again speaking as severely as he could while trying to suppress laughter, said: "Well, I'd bear it in mind after this," and he rode away; but gave a parting shot at the forager as he disappeared: "I hope you'll have a good supper to-night." "Thank you, sir." and he dropped the chickens and saluted the Colonel in true military style.

Now the Colonel could have had the chickens taken away from the soldier, placed him under arrest, and on our return to camp made an example of him for "disobeying orders." The effect would have been that the soldier would have borne it with a dogged indifference, and ever after would have *Efficient reproof.* foraged every chance he got; as it was, the soldier was punished enough. He had been reprimanded by the Colonel before his comrades; there was no chance for him to be defiant about it; and perhaps worst of all, he was expected to have a good supper off the chickens the Colonel knew he had disobeyed orders to get. "Got off easy this time, didn't you?" said one. "Should think I did. Wish to God he'd taken the chickens though," was the reply. No more foraging by that soldier, on that tramp to say the least. This was another instance of "not seeing too much" on the part of the commander. That soldier no doubt had a good chicken stew that night; —— and quite likely he sent a dishful to the Colonel's fire, and probably the dish was returned empty, with thanks; and yet the army was perfectly safe.

What troubles soldiers the most on a march is the want of water, and this is often hard to be borne. Then, again, water obtained on marches is generally vile stuff to drink. We had to get it where we could —from ditches by the wayside, swamps, and sluggish streams; and we had a variety of colors and tastes. *Water.* To offset this we often resorted to the trick of putting a couple of spoonfuls of ground coffee into our canteen of water, and in a short time we had a canteen of cold coffee—at least the coffee taste proved stronger than that of the bad water; and we flattered ourselves that it was better for us.

To go without one meal was passed over as a joke, and we pulled the old waist-belt tighter; but to be without water on a march under a burning sun in Carolina was terrible. When a column is marching it is not so easy to get water as a novice would think. A man will take a dozen canteens, and, leaving his rifle to be carried by a comrade, will start for water. Now if he succeeds in finding water readily, and enough of it, he is very lucky;

—— but even then he has a tedious job to get it, for canteens fill slowly, and when he has them full he has a heavy weight to carry, and does not feel like taking a "double-quick" back to his company. He places the canteens, some over his shoulders to hang on each side, and carries some in each hand; and when he regains the road he finds that the column has been moving all the time, and his regiment may be one, or even two miles away, and he must move faster than his comrades in order to overtake them; so that when he reaches his own company he is certainly more tired than those who stayed in the column. It is this hard work to "catch up" that keeps many from dropping out who really need a rest.

Foot troubles. Another thing that troubles soldiers on a march, especially if it is a forced march or one of any great length, is sore, chafed feet. One might think old soldiers would never be troubled that way, but they are—some more than others, to be sure—but with getting the feet wet in crossing streams and again marching on roads heavy with sand, "which works into the brogans and finds plenty of room," the feet will get sore in spite of the best of care. As a cavalry soldier looks after his horse, so an infantry soldier looks out for his feet; and to obviate this trouble various expedients were tried, such as rubbing the inside of the stocking with soap or tallow, which helped the matter some; but it had to be borne as best it could. The simple changing of the stockings from one foot to the other while on a march, was often a relief to the hot and blistered feet.

As may be supposed, it is not the easiest thing in the world to build a fire while on a march, and in stormy weather; and not every soldier is a good fire-builder, but there were some who could build a fire anywhere and at any time. Nobody seemed to have matches, but they were always forthcoming when wanted, from some place unknown. But it requires a deal of skill and patience to coax the flame of a lucifer into a camp fire. Very few can do it—not more than half a dozen men in a company are good at building fires; and there is most always one who is the boss hand at it. He will build a fire with everything "wet as thunder," and no fuss about it either. He will always find dry twigs somewhere, and his fire is always going first and burns the best. He must have a gift that way.

The same with foraging. Some are "born so."

Building fires.

—— These fellows would make a bee-line for anything in the way of eatables, from any bivouac, in the darkest night that ever "blew." People in the South had a way of burying sweet potatoes in the ground for winter use. These chaps would go direct to these places in the dark, as though they had buried the potatoes there themselves. So with water. I have seen a fellow start as soon as we had come to a halt, take a tin cup and a few canteens, and strike right out into the blackest night, and in twenty or thirty minutes return with plenty of water. He took no thought about it, made no inquiry, but went straight for it, and always was successful. I did not understand it—I do not now; it was, and is to-day to me a mystery. These men were invaluable to a company—they might be called company bummers. Notable among those belonging to Company A were Jimmy Wesson and Moses P. Brown.

Peculiar faculty.

Goulding was the story-teller. Our orderly, Jack Johnson, was also prominent in this line. My stars! How he would tell stories—bring down the house every time. Alas! Poor Jack has gone where—well, I don't think they tell any stories there! Then, of course, there were singers. E. B. Fairbanks,

Storytellers and singers.

T. M. Ward ("Artemas" we called him) and Charles B. Kendall stood here alone. Of course all hands could sing when occasion required, but the three mentioned were *real* singers, with fine voices. And what did soldiers sing? We had old Negro melodies, college songs, and well-known patriotic airs, as well as gems from the operas. But many of the very popular songs we did not have until brought to us by recruits. The last years of the rebellion were much more prolific of war songs than the early period.

Perhaps the most popular were those in which we all could join. "John Brown" was a famous one, and everybody could sing that as all army songs were sung—after a fashion. Then there was that very affecting one, in which all could join if they chose:

Army songs.

>Oh, ain't I glad to git out o' de wilderness,
>Out o' de wilderness, out o' de wilderness;
>Oh, ain't I glad to git out o' de wilderness,
>Bleating like a lamb.

>(*Chorus*) B-a-a-a-a-h! O-o-o-o-o-h!
>Bleating like a lamb, bleating like a lamb;
>Oh, ain't I glad to git out o' de wilderness,
>Bleating like a lamb.

> I went down town in a three ox wagon,
> A three ox wagon, a three ox wagon;
> I went down town in a three ox wagon,
> Bleating like a lamb.
> B-a-a-a-a-h! etc.

There was no end to this song; verses were often made up as they went along.

Another song was:

> Three black crows sat on a tree,
> And they were black as black could be.

Army songs. These lines were repeated by one comrade, and then all joined in—

> One black crow said unto his mate,
> What shall we do for food to ate?

And so on until some one started another. This "round" for as many as chose to join was a popular one, and was usually started by Comrade Goulding. Thus:

> Uncle Abraham, Uncle Abraham,
> Sleepest thou? sleepest thou?
> While the girls are eating,
> While the girls are eating
> Pumpkin pie, pumpkin pie.

And so on, repeating, till all were tired out.

Annie Laurie was a great favorite. Others were Old Hundred, Star Spangled Banner, and Red,

White and Blue, as a matter of course. Comrade ——
Bolster, with his rough, comic songs, always created
much fun around the bivouac fire. Comrade Henry
Goulding had a way of singing a few snatches of
old songs, which always brought a laugh when the
men were tired and cross, and good humor followed.
Here is one:

> Oh, I'd pay ten dollars down,
> And give it mighty free
> If I could only find out
> Who chucked that shell at me.

Army songs.

This is another:

> The corporal stole a chicken,
> And the captain thought it wrong;
> So to punish him he made him
> Pick it all night long.

The quaint humor of Comrade Goulding was really a boon to Company A.

It is amusing to think now how ignorant we all were of soldier life at the start. We had somehow an idea that a soldier must be all the time on the move, marching or fighting; and to be weeks or perhaps months without one or the other was not thought of.

It is interesting to note the difference in the arms we used and those of to-day. Our old Enfield

—— rifles were muzzle-loaders, about five feet long and weighed nine and a half pounds, including a ramrod three feet three inches long, which weighed ten ounces. The whole thing was clumsy and awkward in the extreme. The cartridge was of paper and contained a conical leaden ball weighing an ounce. These cartridges we tore open with our teeth, pouring the powder down the rifle barrel, and sending home the bullet with the paper for wadding, going through the tedious process of drawing and returning ramrod. How different the modern breech-loader with its metallic cartridge, and so light, no clumsy ramrod, no percussion caps, and so easily managed.

Enfield rifles.

Experience taught us that big knives and revolvers were useless lumber for a private soldier, and we soon learned what a quantity of stuff was absolutely worthless for a soldier's use. We will suppose him to be on a march. The clothes he stands in, rifle and equipments, canteen, haversack containing plate, knife, fork and spoon, and his rubber blanket (sometimes a woolen one also), are all the old soldier will carry, and these are often reduced in quantity, for a pound at the start may seem ten pounds before he reaches the bivouac at

Useless lumber.

night. In summer time the scorching sun, and roads heavy with dust or sand made it very tedious marching, while in winter, wind, rain and cold are equally disagreeable.

The distance marched in a day by foot soldiers is often commented upon on account of the few miles traveled. A man, it is said, can walk forty miles in a day. True, a good walker might do it, but he is one man, goes as he pleases, and has no heavy load of rifle, etc., to carry. To march a brigade in a day as far as one man can walk is simply impossible. The more men, the less number of miles traversed. It is good marching for a regiment to travel two miles an hour for the day, and twenty miles in ten or twelve hours is more than the average. A column of cavalry would hardly move over four miles per hour. If the moving column is a large one the regiments in advance may be miles on the road before those in the rear are in motion; and the frequent halts caused by crossing streams, accidents, or for the purpose of rest, are very harrassing to the soldiers in the center or at the rear of the column. The head of the column is the best place to march. The road is clear for one thing, and there are none to stir up the dust; and when the order "Halt"

Distance marched.

—— comes, those in advance have full benefit, for they drop at once to the ground and are getting the rest they all need while the order is running down the line; and by the time those in the rear receive the order the head of the column is moving again. *The best position.* Then those in advance would be more likely to reach their bivouac first, and have their fires built and coffee made before the others, which is a good point; but the regiment or brigade in advance to-day may be in the rear tomorrow, so they even the thing up in a way.

Perhaps a good idea of a column on a march may be had by fancying a dozen miles of road in our own section filled with an almost solid mass of moving men, with batteries intermingled in the line, and ambulances, ammunition and baggage wagons in the rear, while a cloud of cavalry rides on in advance. It is easy to see that the advance would have the best position and the least annoyance on a march.

As the hours go by and the soldiers grow tired, the men so jolly at the start, sober down; and as darkness comes on there is little talking except to growl, and wonder "why in—thunder don't they give us a rest?" and nothing is heard besides but the rattling of tin cups and canteens, and the tramp, tramp of the weary thousands. At these times there is a deal of thinking done—sober thinking about home, its comforts, friends, and the like; and the monotony is broken after a while by such expressions as "Wish I was h-o-m-e." "Me, too." "Same here." "I'm another," etc. Soon some one tells a story, or gets off a stale joke, or strikes up a song, and the spirits of the men lighten up again. Soon comes the welcome order "Halt."

Tired soldiers.

Although we were always provided with cooked rations on a march, still it would happen sometimes that we run short, and then we tried our hands at cooking a bit. Now hard-tack, unless a fellow is pretty hungry, is mighty poor fodder; but we on occasions would improve it in cooking. Various dishes can be made from the omnipresent hard-tack. Soaked in cold water it becomes soft and puffy; now drop it into a pan of hot bacon fat and fry a few minutes, and tell me, if you have been a soldier, is it not a dish fit for a king—if he is a hungry one? Soaking hard-tack in hot water would spoil it—make it leathery and tough. Then we made a sort of pudding of it, and also the "slapjack sublime." Sometimes the hard-tack was wormy (rare ex-

Uses of hard-tack.

—— ception), but that was no detriment, for then we had meat puddings. The inhabitants of the hard-tack were curious creatures—some had legs, some wings, and some had both; and it was very funny to see one try to crawl one way with its legs and fly the other way with its wings. Hard-tack pounded up fine and boiled with bits of bacon, potato, or anything the soldier happened to have, and salted a bit, gave us a sort of skouse—"slosh" we sometimes called it. Skouse, like the mysterious hash of civilized life, was, at times, rather uncertain. I have heard of bits of pumpkin, the wristband of a soldier's woolen shirt, and the heel of a brogan being found in a dish of "slosh,"—'twas not a good season for slosh, either.

Skouse.

A man who has not been a soldier and seen active campaigning does not know what it is to be either comfortable or uncomfortable. What comfort after a hard day's march to come to an early halt in a clear field, fires soon built, coffee quickly made, and all hands to supper. How soon the ground dries off around the bivouac fire. What chatting, joking, laughing is going on—tired of course; but now the pipes are brought to the front—how the boys did stick to their pipes, sorry looking ones, some of

Soldiers' comfort.

them—and what enjoyment they get out of the old briar-woods. Now as the genial warmth spreads around and over the whole circle, tell me, Old Comrade, is it not solid comfort? Or again, in camp, what though it is cold and rainy outside? We have a good, stout canvas over our heads, and a comfortable bunk to crawl into by and by; so let it rain. We are off duty to-night. Poor fellows, walking your beats in the wet, we pity you! We may be there tomorrow, but not now. Light the candles. How cheerful it looks! Around the center-pole stand the rifles; how their bright barrels glisten in the mellow light. The little stove works admirably. Now the pipes, of course. Pass the Killy-kanick; or Billy Bow-legs, is it? How the smoke circles around the pole, filling the top of the old Sibley tent. Here is a comrade writing a letter home; another reading a paper, smoking the while; another is doing a bit of mending; and others are having a game—Old Sledge, may be—with the same old greasy cards that have done duty for so many months. Old Comrade, tell me, is not this real comfort?

The bright side.

The boxes and bundles from home were always a source of great pleasure and comfort to the soldiers.

—— What lots of *things* those boxes held—clothing, eatables, writing materials, thread, needles and such little knicknacks. When a comrade received a box from home it was surely a festal day in that tent. All these were comforts indeed.

But there was another side from all this. What could be more uncomfortable than a cold, cheerless bivouac on the frozen ground, no fires allowed—too near the enemy—consequently no coffee. We munch the ever-present hard-tack in shivering silence, and quench our thirst with cold water from the old canteen. Sleep is impossible, and we move about all through the long, gloomy night to keep from becoming immovable before morning. Again, Old Comrade, is not this in the extreme uncomfortable?

Discomfort.

It is at first thought singular, perhaps, but it is, nevertheless, true, that a private soldier sees and knows little of what is going on around him in battle. If the line is formed and firing has commenced; if he is in his place in the ranks where it is *give and take*, he can see or know only what is going on in his immediate vicinity. He is obeying orders; the enemy are before him; he is loading and firing his rifle as he is ordered to do. He hears the roar of artillery, the solid shot whistle by, and the shells go screeching past, crashing through the trees if any stand in the way. Yes, he actually *sees* these come. He hears bullets zip, zip through the air so spiteful; and he also hears the sickly thud of the ball as it pierces the breast of his near comrade. He sees his companions as they fall around him, and are carried to the rear, or lying at his feet, dying. He sees the gaps made in the lines by the fallen ones closed up again. The noise and confusion at such times are simply infernal. Wild hurrahs break upon the air as some part of the line is ordered to charge; but unless close by he hardly knows what brigade it may be. He hears at last, perhaps, that the enemy are falling back beaten, and that a victory is won; and that is about all there is of it to a private soldier in the ranks. The soldier marches and counter-marches,—why, except from hearsay, he does not understand. Regiments and brigades are pushed about by the commanding general like so many pieces on a chess board, and the soldiers know as little as the pawns of the reasons therefor. Truly, the private soldier's means of knowing about these things are rather limited, at best.

Limited knowledge of military movements.

—— We learned from prisoners what brigades were opposed to us, the names of their commanders, etc. Thus, at Arrowfield Church, we heard from prisoners that Massachusetts and South Carolina had met in a fair combat; that the Twenty-fifth Massachusetts and the Twenty-fifth South Carolina had come together on the bloody field; and we knew, for we had seen it, that the sons of South Carolina had been beaten—scattered like withered leaves. So in all engagements, information is gained from prisoners.

Sources of Information.

. Commanding generals do not usually consult with privates in regard to "what is to be done and how to do it." Still, it is true, a soldier with eyes and ears open, and tongue in his mouth, will pick up a great deal of *hearsay* information from those about him. But of great military movements, or of the movements of any brigade save his own, he can know but little till the thing is done. It doubtless happens, sometimes, that commanding officers drop a few words of information in the presence of some soldier, but of what account is it? It is also frequently the case that regimental officers themselves do not know what is to be done; they are simply obeying orders.

We often hear of men who had rather go into a battle than "eat a good dinner." These men are not found in the ranks as a rule; and wherever found, there is no doubt about it, if the truth is told, they had rather "eat their dinner," and take their chance in a fight later on. "The whistling of bullets was music to his ears" is an expression often used. Quite likely, this; but a deal depends on the distance of the bullet from the ears. If, in passing, it chips off a piece of the ear, somehow the music is not so pleasant as though the bullet was a few rods further off, and it was a piece of some other soldier's ear that was taken. Such talk should be taken for what it is worth, which is very little. *Bravery.*

All men were not equally good at marching. It was not the largest and strongest men that marched the best. Those of lighter build, wiry, kinky fellows, were, as a rule, the toughest, and showed the most endurance in campaigning. *Endurance.*

Of the use of whiskey in the army, I must say that in three years' experience of soldier life, I do not remember a single instance (except in hospitals and cases of sickness) in which it was of the slightest use or benefit to the soldier, or where hot coffee did not serve much better. I have often had the *Whiskey.*

—— boys say to me, "Sergeant, I wish I hadn't touched that whiskey." Coffee was the soldier's friend; whiskey was his foe.

It is true that the soldier may forget until recalled to his mind the hardships of campaigning—the weary night's march, the terrible thirst, the blistering feet. He may forget days of suffering which at the time seemed almost beyond endurance; but the pleasant—yes, happy—hours spent around the camp fire, and at the cheerful bivouac, he never can forget.

CHAPTER XI.

RE-ENLISTING.

AFTER getting comfortably settled in our new quarters at Camp Upton, the boys entered into a new industry for "off duty" hours. They made frequent visits to the wrecks of the frigates *Congress* and *Cumberland*, and obtained bits of copper and wood from which they made rings, pins, crosses and the like. Busy they must be, and this sort of business occupied their leisure time for days.

1863.
Camp Upton.

The month of December passed quietly away. There was enough to do, surely, with guard and fatigue duty, and the regular daily drills. During this month we were reviewed by General Butler. This was his first appearance to us, and we looked at him with curious eyes as the man of whom we had heard so much.

General Butler.

The camp here was a comfortable one, close on the banks of the James river, and our stay was very pleasant for soldier life. January, 1864, opened cold and disagreeable enough, but it mattered not. We were in good quarters, and enjoyed ourselves here.

1864.

Early in December there had been some talk of re-enlisting. Government was offering large bounties for old soldiers to re-enlist, with a furlough of thirty days, they to be known as "veterans," etc. All this was quite tempting, but the idea did not seem very popular among us. Colonel Pickett had explained to the Regiment in his usual short, but clear and expressive way, the whole scheme; and without the slightest attempt to influence the men in any way, told them to think the matter over carefully and decide for themselves. This was frank, open, square and above-board, and what might be expected from Colonel Pickett. The absence of the Colonel during the re-enlistment complications was extremely unfortunate. His application for leave of absence, however, was based upon the belief that the Regiment, being in winter quarters, would remain inactive until early spring; and the re-enlistment scheme, to all appearances, having subsided,

Re-enlisting.

The Colonel's attitude.

he availed himself of the opportunity offered by the Commander of the Department, at Fortress Monroe, of accompanying what was then supposed to be the last detachment of re-enlisted men, to Massachusetts for thirty days. He was utterly astonished, after reaching Worcester, to learn that the re-enlisting fever had broken out again, and that the Regiment was to come home on Veteran furlough.

1864.

Recruits were around among us now who had received sums which seemed to the old soldiers, with their hundred dollars bounty and their thirteen dollars a month, almost fabulous; and when one man proved to us that he had received over twelve hundred dollars down, and would receive his regular soldier's pay too, it set us to figuring up the thing. (These large sums were paid by individuals who were drafted, for substitutes. The draft was being enforced at this time.)

Large bounties.

We were receiving the large sum of thirteen dollars a month. This for three years would be $468., or adding the regular $100. always paid by Government, $568. for three years work, while this fellow received more than double that amount in bounties for the time he might be wanted, one year or two, as the war might last. This was very discouraging to the old soldiers, and many, no doubt, thought more strongly of re-enlisting to get the bounty the Government was offering.

At different times in December, 1863, some one hundred and fifty men of the Regiment had re-enlisted, and early in January, 1864, sixty more. On the 13th of this month the first party of re-enlisted men left on their thirty days' furlough. These men were accompanied by Captain Foster and Lieutenants Daly and Upton. A few days later over one hundred more left, accompanied by Colonel Pickett, Captain Tucker, and Lieutenants Bessey, McCarter and Woodworth. Lieutenant Woodworth had been appointed a recruiting officer, and had had charge thus far of the recruits in the regiment.

With the departure of Colonel Pickett it was supposed by at least the private soldiers, that this re-enlisting business had "played out." Not so, however; the vessel on which the Colonel sailed was hardly out of sight before the talk of re-enlisting began to increase, and the officers openly expressed their wish to take home the Twenty-fifth as a veteran regiment for a thirty days' furlough. To do this, three-fourths of the *duty men* must re-enlist.

One day a printed order was brought to the

Orderly's tent by Sergeant-Major Charles B. Kendall, with the request that it be read to Company A. Accordingly the men were ordered to "fall in," and the Orderly Sergeant, Samuel H. Putnam, read, as required, the order; and "that no misunderstanding might occur," read it carefully the second time. The substance of it was that all men re-enlisting would receive the large bounty offered by the Government (amount specified in the order), a thirty days' furlough, and be known as "veteran soldiers." Those not re-enlisting would be *"permanently transferred to other organizations to serve out their time of enlistment; non-commissioned officers to be reduced to the ranks."* This was plain English, and fell like a clap of thunder on the ears of the men. "Drive us into it like dogs, will they?" "Contemptible." "Tell 'em to go to h—l, Sergeant!" Such were the exclamations heard after the reading of the order. It is unnecessary to say that the Orderly Sergeant made use of some forcible language when he returned the order to Sergeant-Major Kendall.

It has been doubted by some that such an outrageous order ever could have been issued to Union soldiers, though there are plenty of men of "Old

1864.

An astounding order.

1864. Company A," now living, who heard it read and will take oath to it; but to satisfy others, the writer addressed a note of inquiry concerning this order to General Butler, as follows:

WORCESTER, *August* , 1879.
Gen! Ben. F. Butler,
    Lowell, Mass.

Sir: I was a member of Co. A, 25th Reg., Mass. Vols.; and while at Newport News, Virginia, an order was issued concerning the re-enlistment of soldiers, in such terms as these :—'Those re-enlisting should have the large bounties offered, 30 days' furlough, and be known as veteran soldiers. Those not re-enlisting should be permanently transferred to other organizations to serve out the balance of their term of enlistment; *non-com. officers to be reduced to the ranks.* It was my duty as orderly-sergeant to read this order to my company. My statement to this effect, however, has been questioned; and accordingly I wish to know from you if such an order was issued, and by whose authority. This inquiry is made for my own personal satisfaction.

Yours truly,
SAMUEL H. PUTNAM.

General Butler's letter.

General Butler's reply is here given:

WASHINGTON, D. C., *Sept.* 4, 1879.
Dear Sir:

I cannot positively state of my own knowledge by whose authority the order you speak of as to the re-enlistment of veterans was made; but I can say that I knew that such an order was made, and that it was issued with due authority. If it was issued from my headquarters it was only issued by authority of the War Department, and was returned and never objected to by that Department.

1864.

Yours truly,
(*Signed*) BENJ. F. BUTLER.

S. H. Putnam, Esq.,
   389 Main St.,
     Worcester, Mass.

This letter is now in possession of the writer.

This, it would seem, must settle the question. But the order, wherever it may have originated, whether with the War Department or in the fertile brain of Major-General Benjamin F. Butler, was *mean, cowardly* and *contemptible;* and after the departure of Colonel Pickett, Lieutenant Bessey, and those who went home on furlough, the manner in which the re-enlisting was conducted in the Twenty-fifth Regiment, was, if possible, still more mean, cowardly and contemptible.* It did seem as though all in authority had lost their heads. They could hardly praise enough those who would re-enlist, neither could they say enough in censure of those who would not. Officers could be seen almost any time in the tents of the men urging them to put their names down; men were gathered in little groups all over the camp discussing the subject; still not

Nature of the transaction.

---

* Is this strong language? I am responsible.—S. H. P.

—— enough re-enlisted to allow the Regiment to go home on furlough.

1864.

Promises implying promotion were freely made, and every inducement that could be thought of was used. Other subtile agencies were at work, and under their influence some acts were committed that have been a source of regret ever since. The climax was reached when the Regiment was drawn up in line and harangued by the officers, the Lieutenant-Colonel leading off. He spoke of the very liberal bounties offered by the Government for re-enlisted men; of the great benefits to be gained, with no great risk; of the thirty days' furlough; and said doubtless the war would soon be ended, and if a man should happen to lose an arm, he could say he was a veteran soldier and lost it in the service of his country! On the other hand, he consoled those who would not re-enlist by saying they would be sent to Yorktown, which was a very sickly place— a perfect cemetery—and their bones would bleach there with those of McClellan's old mules! He had rather go into battle than go to Yorktown, and he closed by saying, "All the best men are re-enlisting, and there will be nothing left but the *chaff* of the Twenty-fifth Regiment!"—a very unfortunate ex-

Speeches of the officers.

pression, and one that is remembered to this day. The Major followed in very few words, advising them all to re-enlist. Captain Tom O'Neil and others also spoke, and the men were dismissed to their quarters to think the matter over. All this twaddle of speech-making could be brought out if necessary, for there was "a child among 'em taking notes" at the time; but it reads very flat now to anyone who was there.

1864.

The effect of this order in Company A was that not as many re-enlisted as would have done so without it. Some who had thought seriously of doing so now swore they would not under any circumstances. The truth is, the men of Company A were a hard lot to drive or frighten into a measure like this. Prompt to obey, they were just as prompt to defend their own rights (very few in the army), and to express their opinions and stand by them. It is but justice to say that in Company A not the slightest effort was made by its officers to influence the men to re-enlist. Captain Goodwin was at this time on detached service in Massachusetts, Lieutenant Bessey was absent on furlough, and Lieutenant Burr was in command of the Company.

Effect of the order.

"Good God!" said one of Company A, "if Pickett was here he'd stop this wretched tomfoolery," and he would have done so; but Pickett was not there, and the tomfoolery went on. This was all very amusing, but in the eagerness of those in command to carry out their scheme of taking home the Twenty-fifth as a veteran regiment, they overstepped the bounds of justice and right.

Considerable talk there was of *patriotism* during the re-enlisting excitement. Great inducements offered—men re-enlist. With no large bounties, how many would have re-enlisted at this time? Patriotism was it?

On the 19th of January fifty men, and on the 20th, two hundred men were re-enlisted; and as the time appointed for this business had expired, those who had not re-enlisted were ordered to start for Yorktown on the morrow.

The result of all this was that the Regiment was now divided into two factions—"Vets" (veterans) and "Used-to-bes."* Not that there was anything like animosity among us, but there was a sort of *feeling;* and it was plain to be seen ever after,

---

* "We want to go home and be citizens as we *used to be*"—hence the name.

though orders were obeyed as before, that the enthusiasm of the earlier days of the Regiment had departed, never to return.

1864.

On the 21st of January Companies A, G and I, as *companies*, and other members of the Regiment, to the number of two hundred and twenty-five men, left Camp Upton in heavy marching order for that cemetery, Yorktown, under command of Captain Parkhurst and Lieutenants Saul and Johnson, the latter formerly Orderly Sergeant of Company A ("Old Posey"). Doctor Hoyt also accompanied us. As they stood ready to march "I went up and down the line looking into the faces of the men. Firm and resolute they were. Here one in the ranks says: 'Good-bye, Bill,' to one in the camp; 'Good luck, Sam,' from one in the camp to one in the ranks. Shaking hands here and there,—tearful eyes on both sides. It was a sorry sight."

Off for Yorktown

They were thinking men. They had taken in the situation at a glance, had quietly thought over the matter, and had decided they would not re-enlist. Many had families at home, and three years' absence was enough for them. Were they not right? They had fulfilled their contract with the Govern-

―― ment thus far to the very letter, and would to the end. Why should they do more?

1864.

They could not be bought or bribed with large bounties and a thirty days' furlough. They could not be cajoled by honeyed words in promise of promotion or preferment. Nor were they frightened by the harsh words of that contemptible order with its "permanently transferred" and "reduced to the ranks" threats. Neither did visions of that dread cemetery, Yorktown, disturb their slumbers in the least.

Here were men by scores who had been in every fight and on every march in which the Twenty-fifth had participated; never known to shirk a day's duty or shun a day's work; always ready—now kicked out—*the chaff of the Twenty-fifth Regiment.*

The chaff.

To their credit be it said, they always spoke well of their old comrades, and did their best to uphold the honor and name of the Regiment. Under the blue jacket of the private soldier there stood a *man*.

This matter of re-enlisting was simply disgraceful, and is the one foul blot on the otherwise fair escutcheon of the Twenty-fifth Regiment. A man can be a man though but a private soldier; he can be less than a man though he wears the badge of office in the United States service.

It may be said, Why call up these things to-day? "The story of Company A" cannot be told without it. "We should forgive and forget"—how pretty! Forgive is one thing, forget another; the first is easy, the latter impossible.

The order to march was given, and we left Camp Upton about 11 A. M. of January 21st, supposing we had seen the last of it and our old comrades. We had expected, or rather, hoped, that some officer of our own regiment would, *man-fashion*, volunteer to go with us, see what became of us, and stay with us to the end. Here was an opportunity—he would have been one of the most popular officers in the Regiment; but he did not come. We hear much of the love officers have for their men. Was this a specimen of it?

The day's march was a pleasant one of ten or twelve miles, and we bivouacked in the early evening near an old church at Little Bethel. This old church—a mere shell with nothing left inside but the floor—we cleaned out as well as we could, and after supper candles were lighted, a violin found, and a dance started. And such a dance! From

1864.

On our way to the cemetery.

Little Bethel.

1864.

A dance.

—— the outside it was a curious sight—light streaming out of the sashless windows and wide open doors, while rude bursts of laughter were heard from the dancers and lookers-on. It was a weird scene, and rivalled the witch dance in Tam O'Shanter. As the fun waxed furious it was amusing to see the guard, posted by the Captain some time before, come quietly into the building, cooly take off equipments, set their rifles up in a corner, and join in the "all hands round." This was really not according to "army regulations," and might be "conduct prejudicial to good order and military discipline"; but then, what of it? Who were we, anyhow? We were not supposed to belong to the Twenty-fifth Regiment—we had been kicked out of that; and we knew nothing of any other. We were a sort of independent battalion, and we did feel independent. So the fun went on until the candles burnt low, when the dancing ceased, and the guard donned their equipments, shouldered their rifles, and strode out into the darkness to their posts.

The next day the march was continued to Yorktown over miles of McClellan's corduroy roads. We reached Yorktown, a distance of about twelve miles, a little before noon, and here we halted till nearly

6 P. M., when orders were received to push on to Williamsburg, some fifteen miles further. We saw no reason for this; we could have made the distance instead of resting at Yorktown; now it would be an all night's job. But we supposed this to be a part of the great re-enlisting scheme to break us down —twenty-seven miles in one day in heavy marching order; and the cry was raised: "Now will you re-enlist?" "Oh, why did you go for a soger?" *1864.*

Severe march.

This march to Williamsburg was quite a severe one, still there was very little straggling, and about 1 o'clock on the morning of January 23d we reached our journey's end. We bivouacked on the ground, cold and frosty as it was, and slept till broad daylight.

We pitched our tents here, for Companies A, G and I had left Camp Upton as companies, and had tents and all company property with them. Our camp was known as Camp Hancock, in honor of General Hancock, who had fought over this ground. This was near the junction of Queen's creek and York river.

Camp Hancock.

Lieutenant Burr arrived shortly after, and took command of Company A, acting as adjutant. We soon commenced doing picket duty just outside of

1864. — Williamsburg. One day about sixty men of the Eleventh Connecticut arrived here, and were located near us in shelter tents. They had not re-enlisted, —what a bad lot of fellows they must have been! We wondered if they were the chaff of the Eleventh Connecticut.

Camp Hancock was about two miles from Williamsburg, and nearly the same from Fort Magruder, which mounted twenty guns with a ditch around it. The face of the country in this vicinity was dotted with rifle pits, ditches, breastworks, and the like, and was thickly strewn with fragments of arms and equipments, clothing, etc.; and the long lines of *Effects of war.* trenches near Fort Magruder, now sunken, where men by hundreds were buried, showed the terrible struggle the Union soldiers had in taking Williamsburg. It is said they charged three times before the fort was taken, and then it was flanked. At one point in this vicinity ten fortifications, forts, batteries, etc. were in sight.

The country here was fairly wooded with cedar, walnut, chincapin, elm and chestnut. From the river we had oysters, very abundant and large, and we went for them strong. This country is pronounced *very healthy.*

Our second day at Camp Hancock we had visitors from Camp Upton. It appeared they had not yet got the three-fourths necessary of the duty men to re-enlist, and Adjutant McConville and Lieutenant Drennan made their appearance. McConville had not been present during the re-enlisting excitement, and we were surprised to see him here. They tried to talk more re-enlisting to us, but it was no use; and when (in accordance with their orders it was said) they desired Surgeon Hoyt to put as many of us on the sick list as possible, thereby increasing the proportion of duty men at Camp Upton, he laughed in their faces, and said that men who could stand the journey to Williamsburg in heavy marching order, were not very sick he guessed. All this was very queer—it made Captain Parkhurst laugh. He told the visitors they had got into the wrong pew; so they went back to Camp Upton, taking one or two men to re-enlist.

On January 29th Major Mulcahy, of the One-hundred-and-thirty-ninth New York, assumed command. Our own officers left a day or two later; and we were then in a singular situation: two hundred and twenty-five men of one of the best Massachusetts regiments without an officer of their own

1864.

Re-enlisting agents

Officers leave.

1864.
— to command them, wringing words of praise from the lips of the strange officers who were placed over them, and loud in their praise of the Commander of their old regiment, and of the men who composed it. It was a singular state of affairs.

February 4th we broke camp and marched to the camp of the One-hundred-and-thirty-ninth New York, and being drawn up in line, were counted off in lots and assigned to the different companies of that regiment. Some went to their camp, and two lots went into Fort Magruder with Companies F and G of that regiment. This, we thought, was the last act in that contemptible farce of re-enlisting.

Assigned,

The next day at dress parade, Colonel Roberts made a short speech. Addressing himself to the members of the Twenty-fifth, he complimented them on their soldierly appearance, and said he understood the Yankee boys thought they were *permanently transferred* to his regiment, and that the non-commissioned officers were to be reduced to the ranks; this was a mistake, as they were only *temporarily assigned* to his regiment, and would remain only until the re-enlisted men returned from their furlough, when they were to go back to their own regiment. As for non-commissioned officers, he

But not transferred.

had no authority to reduce them to the ranks—their own regimental officers must do that. He would simply request them to do duty with his men in their respective ranks until they did return to the Twenty-fifth.

1864.

This little speech explained the whole matter. We found in Colonel Roberts a man. It is fair to presume that the officers of the Twenty-fifth must have known as much about the re-enlisting as did Colonel Roberts, but concealed it from the men, and set up a scarecrow in the re-enlisting farce. The speech of Colonel Roberts was received with a round of cheers by the men of the Twenty-fifth, in which the New York regiment joined, and for some minutes the Colonel could not be heard. He then stated that a raid was to be undertaken on the morrow in which his regiment was to join, and all must expect a severe march. To the Twenty-fifth Regiment he had nothing to say; they knew their duty and would do it he was assured, though without a single officer of their own. Parade was then dismissed.

Colonel Roberts' speech.

Early morning of February 6th found us in line, and we marched into Williamsburg. When the column was formed it comprised the One-hundred-

1864.

Williamsburg.

——— and-thirty-ninth and One-hundred-and-eighteenth New York, two regiments of colored troops, and I believe but a single battery, all under command of General Wistar. We heard that a regiment of cavalry was to follow us. As we marched through the town it was plain to be seen that it had suffered from the effects of the war; few inhabitants were left; many houses deserted and many burned. William and Mary College, one of the oldest in America, had also been destroyed by Union soldiers in revenge, it was said, for having been fired on from its windows. Though the walls were mostly standing, it was completely ruined. Williamsburg was a still, sunny old place, with one principal street, and our boys, when we left this section, had learned to love the old town for the air of peace and quietness that seemed to hang over it.

About a mile beyond the town we entered the forest, when skirmishers, or rather, flankers, were thrown out, and the column moved on at a good, smart pace till noon, when a halt was made to let the cavalry pass, of which there must have been a regiment, say twelve or fifteen hundred men. From this time the march was quite severe, and began to tell on the New Yorkers. We of the Twenty-fifth however, were used to this sort of business, and worried but little over it. At every halt our boys would drop to the ground and get all the rest there was to be had, and move on at the word of command. Major Mulcahy hardly knew how to take us; he endeavored to keep us on our feet, but it was no go. He talked loud and scolded some. Colonel Roberts, riding up, asked him the cause of the trouble: "Why, you see, Colonel, at every halt these men *simultaneously* sit down." This expression brought out a roar of laughter from the Twenty-fifth boys, in which Colonel Roberts joined. The Major disappeared.

1864.

Major Mulcahy.

For miles after this the soldiers tramped on in perfect good humor. Most of the A boys instead of loading down with rations for three days, figured it thus: four hard-tack for breakfast (with coffee), six hard-tack for dinner (with salt horse), four hardtack for supper (with coffee again)—forty-two hardtack, all told, for three days, which with coffee and meat, was ample, and gave us a light load to carry. We marched rapidly, reaching New Kent, about thirty miles, near midnight; and after *coffee*, and a rest of three hours, were on the road again. About noon we reached Baltimore Cross Roads; here

Rations.

1864. — several roads intersect, one going direct to Richmond, crossing the Chickahominy at Bottom's bridge, only two or three miles distant; others to White House and Charles City.

We struck the Chickahominy river at Bottom's bridge, but the enemy were found there in force, and the bridge had been destroyed; so excepting a little desultory firing, with six or eight killed and wounded, nothing was done, and we returned to Williamsburg, bivouacking one night near what was called the "Twelve Mile Ordinary," where once was a tavern.

Bottom's bridge.

After near three days' absence, not a man of the Twenty-fifth was found straggling; but the New Yorkers kept coming in for twenty-four hours after. We had marched from fifty to sixty miles. Before we broke ranks Colonel Roberts again spoke to his soldiers. He called attention to the fact that while his men were picked up straggling in such numbers, not one of the Twenty-fifth was so found. He also called the attention of officers as well as men to the discipline and behavior of those who, without an officer of their own, could go on a severe march without a straggler, and return in better condition than his own regiment. The truth is, the

No stragglers.

Twenty-fifth boys were right on their "proud," and kept up their dignity and self-respect, and after all had at heart the honor and good name of their old regiment.

The object of the expedition seems to have been to make a stand at Bottom's bridge while the cavalry made a dash at Richmond, liberating prisoners, and burning the city if possible; but, as we have seen, it was a failure.

Our picket line extended from the York to the James rivers, about four miles; and with gunboats on either flank, was a strong one. After our raid, prisoners escaped from Richmond came in often, in squads of from four to six men; and on the 23d of February, five officers came in and reported no enemy between us and Bottom's bridge. A squad from Longstreet's corps came in and surrendered themselves at another time.

One of the picket posts in Williamsburg was at the old brick house once occupied by Governor Page of Virginia. It was built of brick imported from England. The library in this mansion was a room about eighteen by twenty feet, and the walls had been covered with books from floor to ceiling; but now the shelving had been torn down, and the

Old Page house.

1864.

floor was piled with books in wretched disorder —trampled on—most pitiful to see. In the attic of this old house the boys found trunks and boxes of papers of a century past—documents, letters, etc. Among the latter were those bearing the signatures of such men as Jefferson, Madison, Richard Henry Lee; and one or more signed by Washington.

Once more alone.

Early on the morning of February 19th orders came for the One-hundred-and-thirty-ninth to prepare for a march at 7 A. M., with three days' rations. They were sent to Newport News, and we were now alone. The Twenty-fifth boys in Fort Magruder were relieved by a company of heavy artillery, and marched to the old camp of the New York regiment, and we were all together once more. Two lieutenants from the One-hundred-and-forty-eighth New York, whose names I have forgotten, assumed command of the Twenty-fifth men here at this camp, which was known as Camp West; and we were divided into three companies, thus: Company A, Sergeant Putnam; Company G, Sergeant Lee; Company I, Sergeant Moulton; and with the two lieutenants in command we were in good shape. Camp West (named for Colonel West who was in command here) was very comfortable. The men had wooden shanties, while the officers' quarters were very pretty cottages made of upright logs, one story high, most of them, and very neatly fashioned.

1864.

We had not drawn clothing for some time, and when we left Camp Upton many of the men wanted jackets, shoes, and other articles; and the hard service since leaving that camp had put us in bad shape. In some cases men going on duty would have to take the shoes and jackets of those who came off; and thus keep things moving. The New York officers were, naturally, unwilling to be responsible for clothing issued to our men; and non-commissioned officers being of no account, or rather, in a military sense, not responsible parties, of course we could not get clothing, and had to resort to such means as have been mentioned.

State of clothing and arms.

"I one day found some old shoes in a refuse heap, and gave them to one of Company A (Gus Stone, I think) who seemed glad enough to get them." Our arms were beginning to need repairs, but nothing could be done in that respect; still they were always clean and bright, and at the drills we had we received the highest praise from the New York officers.

1864.

Comment of the Inspector.

Towards the close of February an officer from General Butler's headquarters came, as he said, to inspect the Twenty-fifth Massachusetts Regiment; and when the men were drawn up in companies, and for his benefit put through the manual, he expressed great surprise, and pronounced them the best drilled regiment in the Department. When told that these men were simply the "chaff" of the Twenty-fifth Regiment, and had been kicked out of it because they would not re-enlist, his anger knew no bounds. "What is all this? No officers of your own? and on that raid to Bottom's bridge? Why this is outrageous—contemptible. I'll report this at headquarters." Such was his language (I regret I have not this officer's name); and when each company, as inspected, was marched away at his desire under command of a "non-com," who put the men through the evolutions, as wheeling, etc., he declared he never inspected a better drilled lot of men. Very good for the chaff—what must the *better* part of the Regiment have been?

The inspector also said that officers who would use men this way deserved to be cashiered, while every non-commissioned officer on the ground was worthy a commission. . This is not exaggerated a particle. It was written down at the time, and is still legible, though in pencil. It was a strange spectacle—men so well drilled yet so ragged; still there was no complaint, and the men went to their duty cheerfully, and began to look at the whole affair as a huge joke.

1864.

While at Camp West the Twenty-fifth went on several short raids, bringing in families, horses, etc. One morning more men were found in line ready for the march than were reported fit for duty the day before; and the New York officers on inquiry were told that the Twenty-fifth had no sick ones at such times. They said: "Well, we don't understand you Yankee soldiers."

Pluck.

March 2d we were relieved by the Eleventh Connecticut, and on the 3d left Camp West and started for Newport News, reaching Yorktown in the afternoon, and finally halting some distance beyond. The next day we reached Newport News in the afternoon.

Newport News.

While at Camp West we of course made the best of the situation, and an incident I remember as very amusing at the time, was this: Sergeant Wesson ("Rats") with Corporal George R. Brown occupied a small house together. Now when we first arrived

1864. at Camp West, "Rats" noticed a number of fowls running around here, probably left by the New York regiment; and after a deal of pains, managed to catch them all—three or four. "One day I was surprised with an invitation to *dine* with Wesson. The word sounded strangely, but at the proper hour I made my appearance at Sergeant Wesson's cabin, and was met with his 'Hallo, Sergeant, have a seat.' A small table was in the center of the floor, on which were tin plates, cups, knives, forks and spoons, with soft bread and a covered dish. The cabin was filled with an odor extremely pleasant to a hungry man. What could it be? Hog I knew, salt horse I knew, and stewed beans in the old black camp kettle I knew; but what was this savory smell that took me back to the days when we lived in 'God's country,'* and occasionally dined? Can it be? It was—*chicken fricasseed;* and we *dined*. Soldiers sometimes do get a sort of civilized meal."

A dinner.

The country around Williamsburg is cut' up by many ravines, and on one running from the York

---

* A common expression in the army for *home*. Also called "The land of biled shirts."

to the James river, Fort Magruder was built, named for the Rebel general who erected it.

1864.

We were received with much surprise by those of the Twenty-fifth who had returned from furlough, and though they seemed glad to see us, they had hardly expected it. Colonel Pickett returned with the re-enlisted men, and the Regiment was again reunited under his command. During his absence he had been kept in profound ignorance of the unfair and reprehensible methods resorted to for the purpose of reopening the re-enlistment question. But when all the facts came to his knowledge, he expressed in the strongest terms his condemnation, not only of the unjustifiable measures used by the officers left in charge of the Regiment to induce the men to re-enlist, but of the outrageous usage of those who for their own good reasons declined to do so.

Return to the Regiment.

March 22d a severe storm set in, and snow lay six inches deep in camp—rather rough for canvas walls. On the 26th, about 9 A. M., we left Newport News for Portsmouth, and in the afternoon a steamer arrived bringing all the re-enlisted men. So Company A was all together once more, and again there was a Twenty-fifth Regiment.

1864.

There were many recruits brought out at this time, and the Regiment must have numbered eight hundred men. We had been absent from the Regiment about two months. On the 27th of March we went into camp at Getty's Station, which was known as Camp Wellington, in honor of T. W. Wellington, one of Worcester's most patriotic citizens.

Bodies embalmed

While in the neighborhood of Getty's Station we once passed a large tent on which was painted in glaring letters, "Bodies Embalmed," suggesting pleasant thoughts to the soldier. "What do you think of that, fellows?" said one. "How would you like to be embalmed and go home on a furlough?" asked another. "What do you suppose 'tis?" "Well, I reckon it's some kind of a pickle" said another—careless talk of thoughtless soldiers.

CHAPTER XII.

THE BATTLE SUMMER.

1864.

CAMP WELLINGTON was on the railroad leading to Suffolk, and but a few miles from Portsmouth. The tents were nicely pitched when one day a heavy rain came on, and most of those belonging to Company A were completely flooded out.

April 12th, at midnight, Companies A and D had orders to fall in, light marching order, and twenty extra rounds. In a few minutes Company A was in line. The Colonel riding up, it being quite dark, asked, "What company is that?" "Company A, sir" said the Orderly. "Just what I thought" was the response. "He knows Old Company A, don't he?" whispered one in the ranks. Company D soon joined us, and we marched to the station and took the cars. We reached a place called Magnolia

Station, where we bivouacked. The next morning we marched to Suffolk and halted for the rest of the day and again bivouacked. On the 14th, after marching six or eight miles beyond Suffolk and finding bridges destroyed, without even a skirmish we returned to Camp Wellington, reaching there on the morning of the 15th. The whole affair was, it seems, a hunt for guerrillas, in which the other wing of the Regiment took part, going by boat to Smithfield; but the expedition was no great success.

1864.

A raid.

Camp Wellington was not on the best ground that could be chosen, and Company A moved to the rear where the land was higher. "One night —'twas long after taps—we heard water running in our tent, and on getting up to see what the trouble was, found ourselves ankle-deep in cold water. Here was a go. Striking a light, we found the water running through the tent. What could we do? One Sergeant sat on his bunk wringing the water out of his jacket; another on a cracker box was fishing up shoes and stockings from the deep; while 'Rats' Wesson sat on a three-legged stool and sung 'I feel like one forsaken.' It was an uncomfortable 'incident,' but comical. For two hours the rain poured, and then suddenly ceased. 'Rats'

A shower.

procured a shovel, dug a deep hole in the center of the tent into which the water ran, and then bailed out the hole!"

The weather during our stay at Camp Wellington was, much of it, wet and disagreeable; but the boys took advantage of the pleasant days to cut slats in the woods for stockades on which to raise our tents. Dave Bigelow and one man cut two hundred and fifty in one day.

We had heard that Plymouth, N. C., was surrounded by the Rebels, and that General Wessells was besieged there. We were ordered to his assistance, and on the 22d of April embarked for North Carolina on board a steamer—a double-ender—and soon entered the Dismal Swamp canal. This was in part a natural stream and partly artificial, and did not admit of very large craft; was narrow, of no great depth, and very crooked. It afforded a short cut from the James river to Albemarle sound, saving an outside passage around Cape Hatteras. The steamer was provided with iron plates that could be put into position on the sides, affording quite a protection from rifle shots. The Dismal Swamp had been infested by Rebels who had kept up a sort of guerrilla warfare, firing

Great Dismal Swamp.

1864. into boats, and indeed capturing one, so they went armored.

It was bright moonlight as we entered the canal, and we were at once in the forest, for this swamp covers an immense tract of country and is one vast wilderness, having in its center a large sheet of water called Lake Drummond. In many places the stream was so narrow that the trees swept both sides of the boat, and the turns were so short that we were constantly getting aground. The scene as we moved on was one of singular wildness and beauty. Many of the trees were draped with long streamers of gray moss which waved gently in the night air; and the boat moving now in shadow, now in bright moonlight, gave a weird effect to the whole scene, making it very fascinating. We passed a landing where our old friends, the One-hundred-and-thirty-ninth New York, were stationed, and right glad were we to see them—a pleasant surprise for both parties. It was not until the morning of the 24th that we entered Currituck Sound, reaching Roanoke Island about noon of the same day.

Great Dismal Swamp.

We here heard of the capture of Plymouth by the Rebels, so our services were not needed, and the Regiment was ordered back to Getty's Station,

Company A being left on the Island. We found Roanoke as we had left it, except that there were more darky settlers.

1864.

After a stay of three days the Company was ordered back to Getty's Station the same way we came; and leaving the Island on the morning of the 27th of April, reached our old camp at midnight of that day, finding it deserted, the Regiment having been ordered to that cemetery, Yorktown. We occupied the abandoned camp that night, and next day went to Portsmouth where all company property was stored. We left here our knapsacks and woolen blankets, leaving us with only our rubber blankets and the clothes we had on—no more. From Portsmouth we went to Norfolk and took a steamer for Yorktown, arriving at evening of the same day, and the Regiment was again all together.

Our temporary camp of shelter tents was on the York river, some forty or fifty feet above the water. It would seem to be a classic neighborhood for Americans here. We, the "Used-to-bes," had tramped over the fields where the British laid down their arms in the Revolution; we had traced out the lines of earthworks of the contending armies of that day; but of Yorktown little can be said: a very few

Classic ground.

old buildings—and it is doubtful if a house has been built there in the last hundred years. The building occupied by Cornwallis was pointed out, but private soldiers did not have much time to attend to such matters.

Heckman here assumed command of his brigade. It consisted of the Twenty-third, Twenty-fifth and Twenty-seventh Massachusetts, and the Ninth New Jersey. Here the whole corps was reviewed by General Butler.

We were in the First Brigade, Second Division of the Eighteenth Army Corps, General W. F. ("Baldy") Smith. The Tenth and Eighteenth Corps formed the Army of the James, commanded by General Butler.

Our brigade, early one warm May morning, was marched towards Williamsburg a few miles, the Twenty-seventh in advance. The roads were heavy with dust, and we "Used-to-bes" chuckled some to think the whole Regiment had been ordered to visit that cemetery, Yorktown, and was now marching over the same old dusty road we had tramped a few weeks before. We came to a halt about midday, and at 2 P. M. commenced our return march, the Ninth New Jersey leading off; and we reached

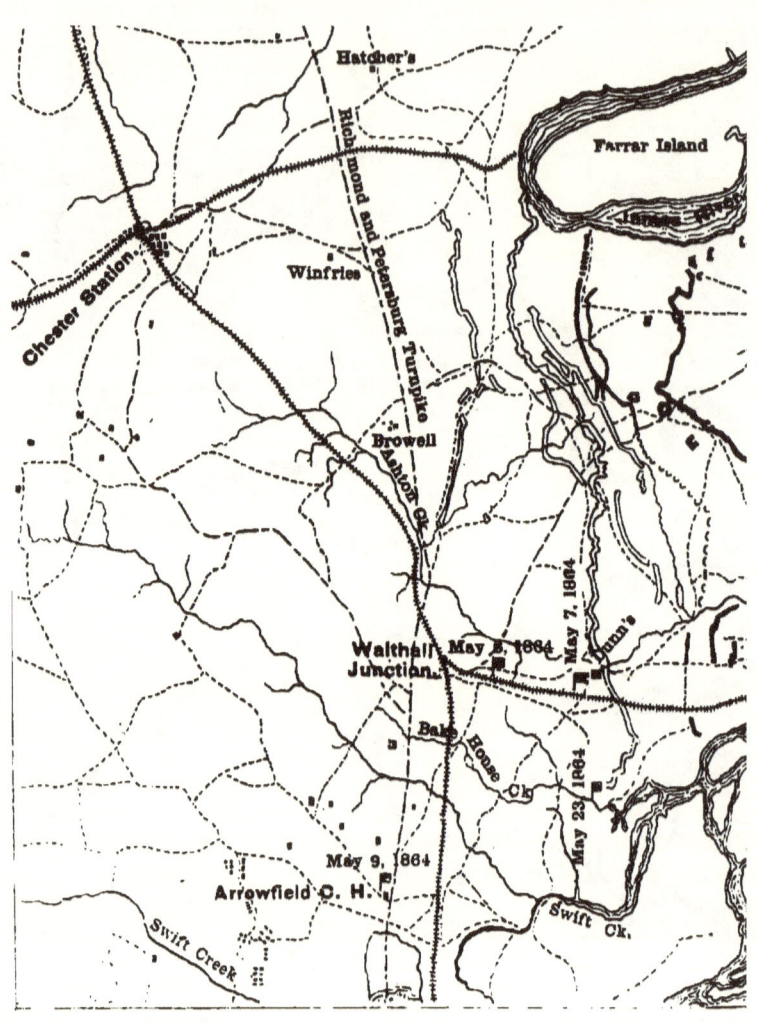

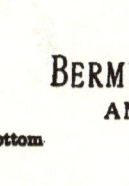

MAP
of
BERMUDA HUNDREDS
AND VICINITY.

一八

our camp pretty well tired out. It seems that all this marching was but a feint, for on the 4th of May we went on board transports with three days' rations, and steaming down the York river, at 5 P. M. anchored at Fortress Monroe.

1864.

Sunrise of May 5th we were on the move again, gunboats in advance, headed up the James river. The day was clear and bright, and the long line of steamers crowded with men, stretching for miles on this beautiful river, reminded us forcibly of our advance on Roanoke Island, and of our departure from Annapolis.

We noticed squads of Negroes running along the banks of the river, with little bundles in their hands, making all sorts of gestures to us as if they would like to be taken aboard—slaves evidently seeking a chance to escape. We passed the ruins of Jamestown and Harrison's landing on our right, Fort Powhatan on our left, and at 5 P. M. reached City Point, at the mouth of the Appomatox river. We here found our old friend, the steamer *New York*, now a flag of truce boat, making trips to Richmond occasionally. We moved still further up the river and arrived at Bermuda Hundred. The troops landed in a very short time, and our brigade was

Up the river.

soon in line, and climbing the steep banks marched through cultivated lands, and finally bivouacked in a field of clover. The night passed quietly away, not a shot being fired.

1864.

On the morning of the 6th we were again in line, the Twenty-seventh men in advance, the Twenty-fifth following. We marched through woods of oak and pine, crossed several small creeks, and reached a considerable hill, up which we moved slowly and cautiously, and on reaching its summit about noon, took possession of "Cobb's Hill" without the firing of a gun.

Cobb's Hill.

The view from Cobb's Hill was a fine one, and very extensive. Looking to the southwest the Appomatox came flowing towards us, and on its banks stood the Rebel fort, Clifton; beyond, and perhaps eight or ten miles distant, were the spires of Petersburg. The whole country around lay spread out like a carpet at our feet, and the scene would have been anything but warlike had it not been for the tramp of soldiers and the rumble of artillery, which continued for hours as the troops hurried by our bivouac. These were the Tenth and Eighteenth Corps which composed the Army of the James.

Cobb's Hill is about eighteen miles from Richmond. It was said that Petersburg could have been taken at this time if our troops had been pushed ahead at once, as there were few Rebel troops in the town. It is easy to tell what "might have been"; but it was not known then how many troops *were* there and if an error was made it was on the safe side, and the capture "was not to be."

1864.

About 4 P. M. we were ordered to fall in, and our brigade, General Heckman in command, with two pieces of artillery, started out on a reconnoissance. We marched down the hill and through woody swamps and fields, a distance of three or four miles, when we heard shots fired in advance which denoted that we had found the enemy. We soon entered a large field and formed in close column by division; some distance ahead was a rail fence, and beyond a railroad, behind the banks of which was the enemy we sought. Company A was sent to the right to act as flankers, and entering a wood on rising ground and coming to a halt, we witnessed with intense interest the movements going on so near.

A reconnoissance.

We saw our boys advance with skirmish line thrown out. The Rebels also sent out their line of skirmishers, and both advanced until it seemed, from our position, that the two lines were not more than five rods apart, and not a shot was fired by either. Meantime our artillery had opened on the enemy, and we could see every shot strike the embankment, —see the dirt fly, rails scatter, and the forms of men moving about. Soon the skirmishers were withdrawn, and the Rebels fired a volley into our boys, wounding some as we saw. The Twenty-seventh opened fire, the Twenty-fifth being held in reserve. The Ninth New Jersey changed their position on the field, receiving a hot fire from the enemy which they soon returned. We saw General Heckman's horse throw up his head and sink down to the ground, dismounting his rider, but the General took the horse of one of his aides, and quietly mounted again. We heard his orders given, and also those of the Rebel commander.

1864.

May 6.
Port Walthal Junction.

We expected to see our boys charge and drive the enemy from their position, but they began slowly to retire; and about 7 P. M. we received orders to rejoin the Regiment. It seems instructions were, not to bring on an engagement, but to find the enemy; this we accomplished, and we reached our bivouac on Cobb's Hill at 10 P. M. The loss to the Twenty-fifth was four killed and fifteen wounded.

This, our first fight in Virginia, is known as Port Walthal Junction.

1864.

May 7th, at 8 A. M., we were again in motion, marching over nearly the same route as before, and found ourselves near the place of yesterday's engagement. On the ground lay our dead, which for some reason—I know not why—had been left on the field where they fell. The bodies had been stripped of their clothing; the enemy could rob the dead, but could not give time to bury them. A party was now detailed to perform that service. Prisoners taken here said the robbery was the *niggers'* work —possible, but not very probable.

Unburied dead.

We found the enemy strongly posted, and our artillery got into position at once, with the infantry at supporting distance laying on the ground in a ploughed field. It was a terribly hot day, and as the hours went by many men were sun-struck. In Company A eight men suffered from the intense heat, three of whom were carried from the field and did not return to the Company for several days.

Chester- field Junction.

Meanwhile an artillery duel was going on, shot and shell flying over our heads as we lay here. It was exciting to watch the enemy's shot as they approached us—they could be plainly seen. At one

1864. — time the Rebels fired chunks of iron rails at us, and these came wabbling along through the air causing a deal of mirth among our boys. We were startled by a flash of light, and a loud explosion: a well directed shell from our battery had penetrated a Rebel caisson, causing the explosion. It was said that when General Heckman saw this he declared that it paid him for the loss of his horse the day before.

May 7. Chesterfield Junction. — On our right we could see General Brooks's division hotly engaged; with loud cheers they dashed forward to fall slowly back. Again they made a charge, and from the artillery we heard the heaviest firing of the day. This time it was a success; Brooks's men drove the enemy, and they withdrew their artillery from our front, and all was quiet in our vicinity. Brooks had destroyed the railroad, taken many prisoners, and a victory had been won. About 5 P. M. we started for our camp on Cobb's Hill. This engagement was known as "Chesterfield Junction."

May 8th we began to fortify Cobb's Hill, and on the 9th, at about 5 P. M., we left our camp, and succeeded in getting as far as the railroad between Petersburg and Richmond without opposition. We destroyed the railroad, broke the telegraph wires, and pushed on towards Petersburg. We encountered a small body of the enemy, and drove them across Swift Creek. Our skirmishers were now firing rapidly, and the enemy opened on us with their big guns; but we pushed forward through woods, and formed in line of battle near Arrowfield Church. The right of the Twenty-fifth rested on the Petersburg turnpike, and at this point was a section of our artillery. We commenced firing at once, as is customary in battle—that is, "at will."

1864.

May 9. Arrowfield Church.

The boys were working like beavers, evidently firing to some purpose; but it was seen that the enemy were about to charge. Colonel Pickett took in the situation, and while we were doing our level best we received the order, "Cease firing," which was promptly obeyed. The men finished reloading their rifles, and stood waiting. We did not understand the "why" of this order, but we soon found out. The enemy were ready, had set up an infernal yell, and were coming at double-quick; but no further order came to us. The Rebels were fast shortening the distance between their line and ours, and we were getting anxious, but finally hear the cautionary command, "Steady, men, wait for the word"; and the Twenty-fifth Regiment stood as steady and

1864.

May 9.
Arrow-
field
Church.

silent as if on dress parade. On came the yelling horde until within—it seemed to us—not over twenty-five yards. It was an anxious and critical moment, and it afforded Colonel Pickett an opportunity to see of what stuff his regiment was made. Suddenly came the order: "Twenty-fifth, ready"; and like clockwork every rifle was in position; "Aim," and every eye was glancing along a rifle barrel; "Fire," and that volley, almost like a single shot, sent death and dismay into that Rebel host.

The effect was like an electric shock. The long line of gray was thrown into the wildest disorder—shattered—broken into fragments. Their men fell by scores, and the ground was literally covered with the dead and wounded of that Rebel regiment. So fierce was their charge that several of their men were actually forced clear into our line and were made prisoners. It was a most gallant charge, and it met with a terrible and bloody repulse.

It was in vain the enemy tried to form for another charge; we kept up such a deadly fire that it was impossible. They fell back out of range, and troubled us no more. Meantime how fared it with our boys? Nobly they stood the shock, but they, too, had fallen by scores. Company A had only twenty-seven men in line at this fight, and of this number nine were wounded—just one third. Many of Company A were on detached service, others sick in hospital, and the Company was smaller than most of the others at this time.

While the fight was going on the smoke from the guns settled thick around us, and the noise was absolutely deafening. As the boys fell out wounded they were taken to the rear and the line closed up, and the firing went on as steadily as ever. How bravely the boys stood up to it! How the sweat rolled off their faces! Lieutenant Bessey was struck in the breast, but fortunately the wound was a slight one. He called for a pipe, and seating himself on a stump, cheered on the boys as if nothing had happened,—no white feather about that man.

Bravery of our boys.

Amidst all the horrors of the situation—dead and dying all around us—an "incident" occurred which shows how the ludicrous and sad are sometimes strangely blended. There was in the Company a new recruit named James Kerwin, a short, good-natured Irishman, who, while the fight was raging, was struck by the fragments of a shell and both legs wounded. Jimmy fell to the ground making the queerest noises, and rolling about so strangely that it was absolutely comical. Sergeant Burr stepped up to him and said: "Is that you, Jimmy? Are you hit?" "Oh," said Jimmy, "oh Sergeant dear, it's me that's hit, and both ov me legs is shpilt intirely." This was too much, and the boys laughed heartily; and the firing went on, ceasing only when the Rebels were out of reach, and all was quiet in our front.

1864.

Jimmy Kerwin.

"The fight was over, and with Comrade Arthur White of Company H (a Leicester boy and a brave one), I strolled over the field, and in our immediate vicinity—that is, directly in front of our regimental line—we counted over seventy dead and wounded, scattered about, and in little heaps of three or four together. From the wounded ones we learned what troops we had been fighting; and it certainly is a remarkable fact that the Twenty-fifth South Carolina and the Twenty-fifth Massachusetts had met in a fair fight." The result we have seen.

Rebel dead and wounded.

It might be thought that with so much firing more men would have been killed and wounded in our front; but it should be remembered that the Twenty-fifth Regiment of 1864 was not the Twenty-fifth Regiment of 1861. It left Massachusetts one thousand strong, but at this time there was not over half that number in the ranks. The regimental line was hardly three hundred and fifty feet long, and it was in front of this line that so many Rebel dead and wounded were found.

The following is a correct list of the wounded of Company A at this battle:

Lieutenant M. B. Bessey, breast.
Sergeant T. M. Ward, leg.
Private L. J. Prentiss, groin (very severe. He died from the effects).
Private Augustus Stone, right arm (amputated).
Private Charles H. Knowlton, hand (three fingers lost).
Private Charles A. Mayers, leg.
Private James White, leg.
Private James Kerwin, both legs.
Private Nelson Tiffany, groin (severe).

Entire loss to the Twenty-fifth Regiment, sixty men.

After the fight parties were detailed to bury the dead as usual. Pits were dug say six or eight feet square, and four or five feet deep, in which the dead were placed as quickly as possible, one row on another, and hurriedly covered with earth—a sickening sight. Yet this is "Glorious War."

1864.

Night coming on cold, we prepared for a cheerless bivouac the best we could. We lay on our arms that night—that is, with rifles by our sides ready to jump into line at a minute's notice. In the morning we were relieved, and fell back to our camp on Cobb's Hill. This battle took place near the old weather-beaten building known as Arrowfield Church, from which the battle takes its name.

On the 12th of May we were ordered off again in light marching order. Many boys left their rubber blankets behind; this proved a mistake, for we were gone five days, every one of them cold and wet. The rubber blanket should *always* go with the soldier, and the woolen one too, if possible. During these cold, wet nights we suffered a great deal. We had more or less fighting every day.

Again in motion.

The first day we discovered the enemy about noon, and drove them across Proctor's Creek, and halted for the night in the edge of a wood. On this day, while lying on the ground in line, Comrade William Holman was struck by a bullet intended, no doubt, for a mounted officer riding in our front. This was the only bullet that reached us at this time;

Death of Holman.

and if we had been *standing* in the same place probably Holman would not have been hit. He moaned pitifully, was taken to the rear, where he soon died, and we saw him no more.

1864.

The next day (May 13th) we were ordered forward, and entering a thick wood, the Regiment marched through in line, the skirmishers encountering the enemy's pickets and driving them to their works at Drewry's Bluff. On reaching the edge of the woods we were in sight of the enemy's entrenchments, and received their fire at once.

We were ordered to lay down, and for hours we had shot and shell flying over us. Many of the boys went to sleep in this situation, undisturbed by the noise of the firing. Once a shell burst directly over our line, and inquiry was made if anyone was hit. Some raised their heads and looked about, but hearing no reply, curled down again; and it was not known until some time after—certainly more than an hour—that Comrade Henry Goulding was killed. A portion of the shell had struck him on the back between the shoulders, killing him instantly. He died without a groan.

Death of Goulding.

Skirmishers were thrown out, and succeeded in keeping the enemy's guns pretty quiet for two days

1864. (oh fatal delay), though more or less firing was going on all the time. We had changed our position, and were now nearer the enemy's works than at first, behind a weak line of breastworks made of logs, rails, and earth thrown up with bayonets and tin cups, for we had no intrenching tools.

On the 15th our brigade held the right of the army, and the regiments were in line in this order: extreme right, Ninth New Jersey; then followed the Twenty-third, Twenty-seventh, and Twenty-fifth Massachusetts. The space between the Ninth New Jersey and the James river was .occupied by a few colored cavalrymen. During the night of the 15th there were several attempts to break through our line, which were repulsed every time with severe loss to the enemy. Later a heavy fog settled down over the whole country around, so dense that at a distance of two or three rods nothing could be seen.

May 16. Under cover of this fog, about 4 o'clock on the morning of the 16th, the Rebels made an attack on our right, and, after heavy fighting, succeeded in crushing the Ninth New Jersey, and turning our right; and before we were aware of it, had gained our rear. At the same time we were engaged in front, an assault being made along our whole line.

Battle of Drewry's Bluff.

In this horrid gloom, the yells of the advancing enemy, the musketry firing, and the roar of the artillery, were sounds terrible to hear, and madly exciting. Soon the regiments on our right came rolling down upon us, crushed and broken. The Twenty-fifth gallantly repulsed the impetuous charges of the Rebels in front, and unflinchingly held their position *alone* after the whole line, right and left, had been broken and swept away by the overwhelming force of the enemy. Lieutenant Daly, in command of the right flank, Company K, reported the perilous condition of affairs on the right, but the Colonel replied that he had no orders to retire, and that he proposed to hold on at all hazards. He directed Daly to deploy his company to the rear at right angles with our line, and check the flanking force. The Rebels advancing in large numbers, immediately overpowered and captured most of his company.

Company A, under command of Lieutenant Burr, was now ordered to the rear as skirmishers, to check, if possible, the tide which seemed about to overwhelm us. We soon saw dimly through the fog forms of men moving about, and, approaching nearer, noticed that some had on blue coats ; and

1864.
May 16.
Battle of Drewry's Bluff.

In peril.

<small>1864.
May 16.
Battle of Drewry's Bluff.</small>

—— supposing they must be our own men, one of Company A sung out: "What regiment are you?" "We are Rebels, damn you; take that!" was the reply; and the whistling of bullets told us what they meant. "Good for you, Johnny; take it back again," was the retort of the A boys, with the same accompaniment. But of what use was it? We were a thin line of skirmishers, and it was plain to be seen that there was at least a regiment in front of us. We soon, obeying orders received, quickly moved off by the right flank, narrowly escaping capture.

The enemy advanced and opened fire on the Regiment at not over twenty yards distance. This was indeed a most critical moment. Hotly engaged with the enemy in front, and now receiving a heavy fire in the rear, the Regiment was simply surrounded. There was a single chance left. Instantly we were faced to the rear and ordered to charge; and with a cheer the Regiment rushed upon the Rebel line, pouring a deadly volley into their ranks, and throwing them into such disorder that before they could be rallied by their officers our Colonel had given the order: "By the right flank; and we had marched around the enemy's left to the rear, ready for them again upon anything like equal terms.

<small>A charge to the rear</small>

The conduct of the Twenty-fifth at the Battle of Drewry's Bluff was magnificent and beyond all words of praise. The perilous position they were placed in was a trying test of their courage and soldierly qualities; and nothing but their excellent discipline and prompt obedience to orders saved the entire Regiment from capture. Cool and undaunted they waited for orders, and they received them. They had unqualified· confidence in their commander, and to his prompt and decisive action they owe their marvelous and brilliant escape.

1864.

But Company A did not all escape, as the following list will show:

Loss in the battle.

Corporal Walter H. Richards, killed.
Private John A. Coulter, wounded.
Private Francis Greenwood, wounded.
Corporal Jerome H. Fuller, captured.
Private Amos E. Stearns, captured.
Private Charles E. Benson, captured.
Private B. C. Green, captured.

Comrades Goulding and Holman had been killed two days before, so, all told, Company A lost nine men in the fight at Drewry's Bluff.

In this fight we lost our brigade commander,

General Heckman, who was taken prisoner. Captain Belger, with a portion of his battery, was also captured. Our brigade (1st) had lost, since we landed at Bermuda Hundred twelve days before, almost eleven hundred men. The Twenty-fifth Regiment in the same time lost over three hundred men, while Company A lost eighteen.

1864.

Heavy loss

General Heckman, and Colonel Lee of the Twenty-seventh, both being captured, the command of the brigade devolved upon Colonel Pickett, leaving Lieutenant-Colonel Moulton in command of the Twenty-fifth. Colonel Pickett rallied the brigade, forming line of battle half a mile to the rear of the original line in the morning. During the day different positions were occupied, holding the enemy in check. About 5 P. M. we fell back towards our camp at Cobb's Hill, which we reached at 10 o'clock.

General Stannard, a few days later, assumed command of the brigade, and Colonel Pickett again took charge of his own regiment.

An "incident" occurred during the fight at Drewry's Bluff that was highly amusing. Private Sidney Atkinson, a tall Yankee recruit, during the struggle in the fog was taken prisoner by a squad of Rebels. He had been in the habit of carrying, attached to

An incident.

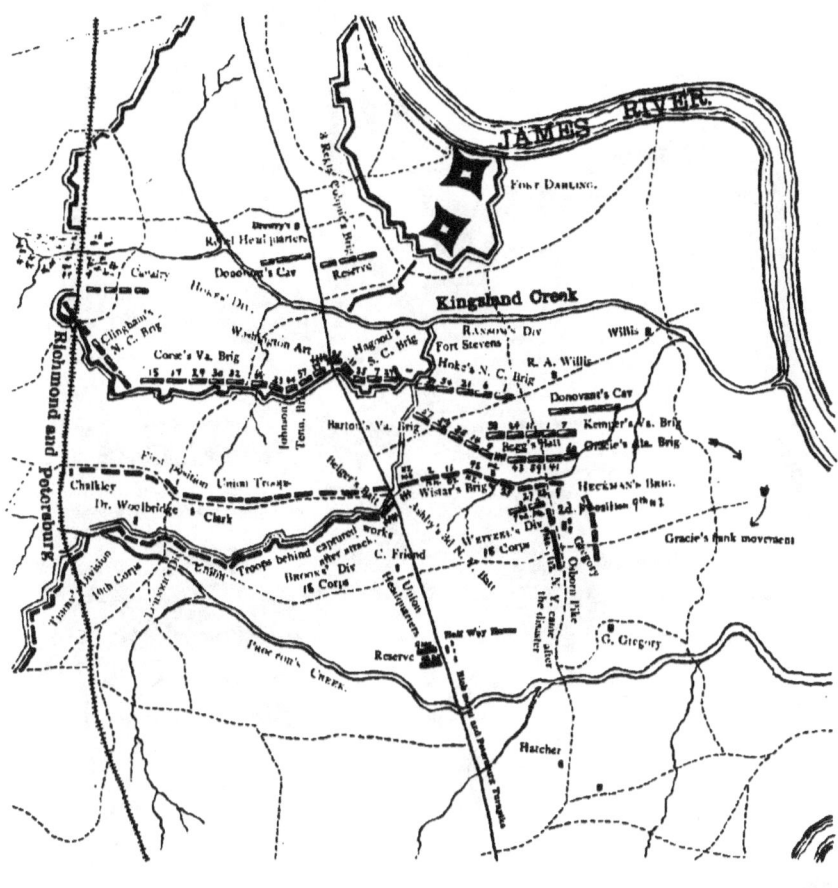

Battle-field of Drewry's Bluff
May 16, 1864.

his belt, a small hatchet; and when taken prisoner almost the first words said to him by his captors were: "Well, Yank, I *reckon* we'll take that hatchet." Atkinson replied: "I suppose you will, Johnny," and gave it up at once. He noticed as they marched along that his captors had lost their way in the fog and were trying to find their men. Atkinson cooly said: "Look here, Johnnies, I was over this ground this very morning. I know where we are and where your men are. I'll show you; come on." He quietly led off, his captors as quietly following; and in less than two minutes he led them into the presence of our own men. The Rebels saw the joke at once, and cursed their "damned stupidity." "Now, Johnny," said Atkinson, "I *guess I'll* take that hatchet"; and he did.

The tables turned.

The following extract from a letter of Captain Emerson Stone of Spencer to the writer, shows that the promise made by the prisoners captured by us at Roanoke Island in 1862, to make return for our kindness to them while in our hands, if it was ever in their power, was not forgotten:

1864.

Kindness repaid.

I was captured May 16th, 1864, by "Wise's Brigade" of Virginians, the same men who surrendered to us at Roanoke Island in '62. My captor was a tall, fine-looking man, who on learning what regiment I belonged to, at once declared his intention of standing by me, and doing for me all that was in his power to alleviate my sufferings, this in pursuance of a resolve formed, as he said, by their entire brigade after their exchange at Roanoke, to treat thereafter every Yankee that the fortunes of war might throw into their hands with the greatest possible kindness, in repayment of the courteous treatment which they received at our hands as prisoners of war. Right royally did he fulfill his vow, for no one could have showed greater kindness than he showed to me. He bound up and stanched my wounds at first, then brought water to refresh me, placing at the same time the contents of his haversack at my disposal; protected me from the covetous desires of his needy comrades, who sought to replenish their long neglected wardrobes at my expense; and in every way seemed anxious to show his sympathy and willingness to help me.

Reaching the hospital he asked the surgeon in charge to look at my wounds, and secured his early services, as well as a special guard detailed to care for me and look after all my wants until the surgeon called for me. Then taking from his shoulders his own blanket, he carefully placed it under me, and after arranging me as comfortably as possible, said he was obliged to report to his command, and bade me a feeling good-bye. I have often regretted that I did not learn the name of this whole-souled man whose large heart was filled with humanity, although covered with the Rebel "gray"; and I would to-day, after the lapse of so many years, give the best hundred dollars I ever saw for the privilege of grasping him by the hand.

I will add that I subsequently received the same kind treatment from the surgeon who amputated my arm, who was also a kind-hearted man; but I have always surmised that his interest in me was stimulated by the words or efforts of my kind captor, who so faithfully stood by me—an enemy—in my hour of sore distress. Do not wonder that I have a kindly feeling for Wise's Brigade of Virginians, and especially for my unknown generous captor, and that I often breathe for him a prayer for heaven's richest blessings.

1864.

General Heckman has claimed, in a letter published in a Northern paper, that the Rebel loss in our front at Drewry's Bluff was estimated at over four thousand, which was many more than our brigade numbered. He also stated that the musketry firing was the severest he ever experienced. Our prisoners all reported the slaughter in our front as something terrible and unparalleled.

Statement of Heckman.

For some days the troops were engaged day and night in strengthening our fortifications at Cobb's Hill. Almost daily the Rebels made an attack on some part of our line, but were easily repulsed. All this time we lay on our arms at night, and were turned out at two or three o'clock in the morning, ready for an attack. In one direction from our camp was a beautiful grove, but it was in the way of our guns. Pioneers were sent into this grove, and in forty-eight hours it had disappeared. In forty-eight hours more a heavy line of earthworks extended over the spot, and cannon looked down into the valley below. These works reached from

On the defensive.

1864. the James river to the Appomatox, below Port Walthal.

This work continued until the 27th of May, when orders were received to move again, so we marched a few miles and bivouacked for the night. The next day we moved to City Point, crossing the Appomatox over a pontoon bridge; and once more going on board transport steamers, were soon sailing down the James. We reached the York river, and passing up that and the Pamunky, arrived at White House Landing May 30th.

A delightful sail. The weather was fine as we sailed down that beautiful stream, the James; and the entire trip to White House Landing was in striking contrast to what we had been through of late. The York river is much smaller than the James, but still a noble stream, while the Pamunky is so crooked that a vessel will sail towards all points of the compass in making the ascent.

On the 31st of May we marched all day, and about midnight, while passing through an extensive forest, we ran on to the pickets of Grant's army. *Army of the Potomac.* He had been fighting his way through the Wilderness, and we had, at last, joined the ARMY OF THE POTOMAC.

Our march from the White House was through a good country, reminding us of New England. By the roadside we passed grape vines, cedar, shrubbery of oak, and blackberry bushes—much like the country roads in Massachusetts.

1864.

June 1st opened as fine as could be desired, but by the middle of the day the heat was intense, and many soldiers were completely exhausted by the march. For many miles the road, which was heavy with dust, had been strewn with dead horses and mules, and the stench from them was horrible. About 4 o'clock in the afternoon we found ourselves before the enemy's intrenchments at Cold Harbor.

Severe march.

June 2nd our brigade was under fire nearly all day, and at night the enemy charged our lines, but were repulsed with a heavy loss. Our army was in line at this time in the following order: Ninth Corps (Burnside) on the right, then came the Fifth Corps (Warren), Eighteenth Corps (Smith), Sixth Corps (Wright), and on the extreme left the Second Corps (Hancock). Sheridan with his cavalry covered our left at the Chickahominy river, while Wright's cavalry guarded our right. The line of battle at Cold Harbor was six miles long.

Battle of Cold Harbor.

1864.
June 3.

Rations and ammunition were given out, and we laid on the ground that night to get what sleep we could, for "there was to be terrible work on the morrow." June 3d was a black day in the calendar of the Twenty-fifth Regiment.

We left our bivouac in the early morning, moved a short distance, and laid down again under cover of thin woods. We had caught glimpses of the enemy's earthworks, and saw their immense strength. We felt that it would be almost an impossibility to take the works in our front. We knew that behind those works were thousands of brave men with rifles, awaiting our approach; and we knew those intrenchments were lined with batteries. We knew it meant slaughter for us to make the attempt; and gloomy forebodings settled down over the whole regiment. The Twenty-fifth at this time had only three hundred men in the ranks, and the whole brigade of four regiments numbered scarcely fifteen hundred men.

Before the battle.

All these things we talked over as we laid on the ground under the trees. A little ravine was near, through which flowed a small rivulet—a mere thread of water; and we were partially protected by a slight elevation on our right. We calculated the chances, and we felt that they were terribly against us; but to "obey orders" is a soldier's duty. "Wait for a time to die!"

*1864.
June 3.
Battle of Cold Harbor.*

We were in close column by division at this time —that is, a front of two companies in a division— five divisions. We heard loud cheering on our left, and artillery firing rapidly. We knew our boys were making an assault on the enemy's line. We could only guess at the result. An officer passed by and reported Hancock successful.

"Forward!" The hour had come. We moved slowly up the slight elevation, beyond which a thousand deaths awaited us. No man faltered, and only the wounded ones fell out; for we were under fire all the time while lying under the trees. We gained the front and were obliged to oblique to the right somewhat, to place us in proper position. We were at once under a murderous fire. The enemy's works were directly in front. Colonel Pickett was marching at the head of the Regiment, and at this moment waved his sword over his head, and shouted his orders: "Come on, boys; forward, double-quick. CHARGE!" We dashed forward with a cheer. The enemy's earthworks in our front, perhaps twenty rods distant, were enveloped in

The charge.

1864.
June 3.
Battle of Cold Harbor.

—— smoke and flame, and volley after volley of musketry sent bullets through our ranks like hail. At the same moment we received an enfilading fire of artillery on both right and left flanks.

The slaughter was fearful. Colonel Pickett went down with a bad wound in the hip, and the ground was thickly covered with the dead and wounded—

The result. and so quickly done. The enemy kept up such an incessant fire that to stand up against it and live was impossible. So to escape utter annihilation we dropped to the ground and stubbornly held the position we were in, and—an actual fact—with tin cups, knives, bayonets, and our hands, threw up, painfully and slowly, a low bank of earth, which in a measure protected us from the enemy's fire; and the hours dragged slowly along until dark, when intrenching tools were brought, and regular earthworks were made and rifle pits dug.

Brigadier-General P. D. Bowles of the Confederate Army, in a letter printed in the Philadelphia Weekly Times of January 31, 1885, describes this charge of the Twenty-fifth as he saw it from the Rebel intrenchments. His account is as follows:

On looking over the works I discovered what I supposed to be one regiment, with a single flag, and an officer in front with sword raised high in the air, calling on his men to charge. I ordered my command to place their guns on the works and wait for orders. When the advancing line reached within seventy yards I ordered my line to fire, when the whole of the Federal regiment fell to the ground save one man, who ran back to the edge of the woods and attempted to hide behind a white oak tree, but was completely riddled by fifty balls in less time than it takes to write it.

1864.

Confederate testimony.

The heroic regiment that made this gallant charge was the Twenty-fifth Massachusetts, which was the only regiment that obeyed orders to advance. This we learned from the twenty odd officers and men who fell down among the dead and wounded at the first fire. The balance of the brigade had refused to go forward, and not since the charge of the three hundred at Balaklava has a more heroic act been performed.

In this charge of the 3d of June the Twenty-fifth Regiment lost, in killed, wounded and missing, two hundred and twenty men out of three hundred and thirteen, leaving for duty, June 4th, less than one hundred men, Company A losing fifteen out of thirty. All this happened within a few minutes of time, for nearly all fell during the charge.

The following is a list of the killed, wounded and missing of Company A:

Killed: Private F. B. Brock.
    ‘‘   Ira Lindsey.
    ‘‘   Sidney J. Atkinson (he of the hatchet).

1864.

Loss at Cold Harbor.

Wounded: First Lieut. M. B. Bessey, shoulder.
Second Lieut. Geo. Burr, head.
First Sergt. S. H. Putnam, slight.
Sergt. Frank Wright, side.
Corporal G. F. Stearns, hip.
" " L. J. Elwell, shoulder.
Private L. W. Stone, severe.
" " A. D. Whitcomb, head.
" " J. Madden, groin.

Missing: Corporal Walter S. Bugbee.
Private H. W. Dryden.
" " Charles O'Neil.

Colonel Pickett.

The wound of Colonel Pickett was a very severe one, and he was absent from his command for several months. He rejoined the Regiment at New Berne in November, 1864. He was then suffering severely from his wound, and being disabled from further duty "Our Captain" left the service in January, 1865, with the rank of Brevet Brigadier-General, this honor having been conferred upon him for gallant and meritorious services during the war.

The 4th of June was passed quietly behind the works, but on the 5th there was fighting all day long. At this time the stench from the dead bodies between the opposing lines was dreadful. Parties were sent out at night, and in the darkness and silence tried to bring in the wounded. A flag of truce had been sent to the enemy before this, to make arrangements to bury the dead, but with no success.

On the 7th cannonading was kept up all day, and men were killed at times, half a mile in the rear of our works. A second time a flag of truce was sent, which was successful, and fatigue parties went out from both sides, and the dead were buried. While this was going on there was no firing along the lines, and the stillness that ensued seemed very strange to us. The truce was only for two hours, and it was a hurried job, this burial of the dead. It was a singular spectacle as we mounted on top of our earthworks and looked over the ground. The Rebels did the same while the burial of the dead went on. When the time was up a signal gun was fired, and the detailed parties made haste back to their respective places; and *then* it would have been death to show a head above either line of works.

The 8th of June was a beautiful day, but very hot and severe for the boys in the rifle pits. At night

1864.

Burial of the dead.

1864. —— the military bands of both armies played. The Union bands played The Star Spangled Banner, Red, White and Blue, and Yankee Doodle, while the Rebel bands gave us Dixie and The Bonnie Blue Flag.

The 9th, 10th and 11th of June passed away without actual fighting, but a constant firing was kept up.

The Twenty-fifth had landed at Bermuda Hundred on the 5th of May with seven hundred splendid veterans. One month's fighting in the rear of Richmond reduced this number to a trifle over three hundred; and the morning after the Battle of Cold Harbor (June 4th) there were only one hundred men fit for duty. "The gallant six hundred," where were they? Killed, wounded, in hospital, and down in Southern prisons. This was war and its deplorable results. It was a terrible sacrifice, but it was for the Union and the flag, and our country was saved by the blood of its heroes.

Fearful sacrifice.

It was now ebb tide with the Twenty-fifth Regiment. Six officers and less than one hundred men were all that remained for duty. This shows the wear and tear of regiments and brigades in active service—that terrible drain of men going on constantly, and which all the recruits could not replace.

<small>1864.</small>

One day, at Cold Harbor, Lieutenant George A. Johnson of Company G, formerly Orderly Sergeant of Company A (Old Posey), was wounded in the rear, and a stretcher was called to take him away. He was carried slowly a short distance, and as the bullets were flying thickly around, he became uneasy, and finally jumped off and made a straight line for the rear, saying: "I can't wait for no damned stretcher." As he passed along on his way to the hospital tent, with blood streaming from his wound, he met the commanding general, who said: "Lieutenant, don't you want a stretcher?" "I've got one coming," was the reply. "Are you badly wounded?" "Nothing but a shot in the *rear!*" said Johnson; "Guess it won't amount to much!"

<small>Another incident.</small>

It would hardly be fair to pass by the "Dog of the Regiment" without some notice. When the Regiment left Worcester Company A had two puppies as pets. They were christened Whiskey and Brandy, and were well cared for. Brandy was a good dog and died young, but Whiskey, on the contrary, continued to thrivë, going out with the pioneers at New Berne, going on marches with the

<small>Our dog Whiskey.</small>

1864. Regiment, and participating in nearly all the battles to Cold Harbor. At this battle the dog was wounded by a rifle ball, and found his way to the hospital, where the ball was taken out and given to the Orderly Sergeant of Company A. Whiskey was well cared for at the hospital, but in the movement of troops after the fight the poor dog was lost, and we never saw him again.

The Company A boys taken prisoners at Cold Harbor fell into the hands of North Carolina troops, some of whom were among those captured by us at Roanoke. On learning what regiment our boys belonged to these men treated them with all possible kindness, and nobly redeemed the promise made while our prisoners, to make return for our kindness to them if they ever had the opportunity.*

Works evacuated Sunday, June 12th, passed very quietly, with no more firing than usual. Captain Goodwin, who had returned a few days before, was now in command of Company A. After dark the boys were called in from the rifle pits, and we quietly evacuated our works; and marching all night, reached White House Landing about 5 o'clock on the morning of the 13th. This night march was a very hard one,

* See page 90.

and on reaching the Landing, guns were stacked, the boys dropped to the ground, and many were instantly asleep. Some crawled on their hands and knees to the river's brink, two or three rods away, and drank like so many animals. They were completely exhausted.

1864.

We went on board transports again and steamed down the crooked Pamunky and the York, up the James, landing at 9 P. M. of June 14th near our old camp. Four days' rations were cooked, and on the morning of the 15th, at 4 o'clock, we started off on a march. This was surely active campaigning.

Active campaigning.

On the 15th we encountered the enemy, and our regiment having the right of the brigade, had an open corn field in our front. We marched in line of battle to within perhaps three hundred yards of a Rebel battery situated on a hill to our left, and came to a halt. The enemy opened on us at once with both musketry and artillery. They had our exact range, and we had one man killed and eighteen wounded in a few minutes. Captain Goodwin was wounded by a shell which exploded very near his head, hitting him in the shoulder and in the face, from the effects of which he lost an eye. This shot came from the right, and not from the

Encounter with the enemy.

Captain Goodwin.

1864. —— battery on the hill at the left. This was the last we saw of Captain Goodwin in Company A. He was mustered out the following October as Brevet Major.

Captain Parkhurst moved us forward at double-quick about one hundred yards. This movement took us out of range of the enemy's guns, and though men were still wounded here, it doubtless saved many lives. Lieutenant Bessey was hit once *Bessey's wounds.* more, this time in the foot, making three hits for him within a few days. Though Dame Fortune scatters her gifts with a lavish hand, in battle she distributes them very unequally. Some are never wounded, others always are. Lieutenant Bessey was hit four times—yea, a fifth time was he *touched* (which, by the way, was scarcely mentioned in the dispatches); yet with all this, and added to it the old army saying: "Three times and out" (death), Bessey served through the war, and preserved that good nature for which he was noted. Bessey was irrepressible. He was mustered out as Brevet Major in March, 1865.

We were ordered to lie down, and all day long we were in this corn field under a scorching sun, with no protection save what we obtained by pulling up the corn, which was about two feet high, and covering our heads with it. It was provoking to lay there as we did, hour after hour, and hardly fire a shot in reply to the Rebels, who were blazing away at us all the time. They would give us a few shells, then a solid shot would come roaring along and plough up the dust near us, then the rascals would get outside their works and fire at us with their rifles. We kept the enemy busy in this way while our troops got their guns into position.

About sundown we heard a heavy gun fired on our left, and looking at the Rebel battery saw a shell burst directly over it. Another shot was fired, then many in quick succession, and shells exploded thick and fast in that battery. The whole Regiment got up and watched with intense interest the movement now going on. Soon a long line of Boys in Blue was seen moving towards the battery. The line was somewhat broken as the boys made their way through the trees, which had been cut down and left to obstruct the way; but they passed through them, and with wild cheers swarmed up the hill like bees. Shells from the Union guns were dropping into the battery every moment; the Rebels attempted to reply, but it was of no use; the place was too hot for them. Soon the Boys in Blue

1864.

Battle near Petersburg.

1864.

Battery taken.

We advance.

reached the enemy's works, and over they went on one side while the Rebels departed over the other. Our Regiment cheered enough to split their throats. Then the guns of the battery were turned on the flying enemy, and the fort was taken. Down went the Rebel rag and up went Old Glory. Nine guns and two hundred prisoners were reported as the result of this gallant movement.

A little later, just at dark, an advance was made, and Company A was thrown out to join the skirmish line already moving on our left, under command of the Orderly Sergeant, S. H. Putnam, all three of the officers having been wounded. While advancing at double-quick, solid shot from some Rebel guns directly in front came over the line, but did no harm. A battery in this direction had made some trouble during the day—probably Captain Goodwin was hit by a shot from it.

Still advancing, an earthwork was seen directly in front; but the order was "Forward!" and away the boys went over the breastwork, all together, fortunately finding the battery deserted. It had evidently been vacated but a few minutes, and in a great hurry, for blankets, clothing and equipments were scattered around, and a supper already prepared was left untouched. We found here two brass Napoleon guns, and caissons complete. Word was sent by Corporal Jimmy Green to Captain Parkhurst, commanding the Regiment, who ordered Captain Harrington with his company to draw the guns to the rear, which was done. This capture was represented in the papers of the day—New York Tribune and others—as having been achieved by Captain Harrington and his company, when really the guns were taken by Company A under command of a non-commissioned officer. The Worcester Spy printed a letter giving a statement as above, signed by one of the members of Company A. When this paper reached the camp Captain Harrington accused our Orderly Sergeant of writing the letter, and claimed the great honor of having captured the guns, he, as he said, being a commissioned officer, and the skirmishers being under command of a non-com. The officer claimed it because he *was* an officer; we claimed it because we *did* it. The affair was of no great importance anyway; but if there was honor enough for an officer to claim, there was certainly enough for a few privates; for the achievement was theirs, and theirs only. So much for the taking of these guns; and simple justice requires that to

1864.

Capture of the guns.

The truth of it.

Company A should be given the credit which is, most certainly, its due.

1864.

Before Petersburg.
June 16th Company A numbered one sergeant, one corporal, and eight privates fit for duty. From this time the Regiment performed duty in the fortifications then being constructed before Petersburg.

On the 16th of June, strange to say, the Regiment was quiet all day, but at night fell into line and marched several hours under fire, getting back to our bivouac at midnight. The 17th was another quiet day; we moved about two miles, still under fire. On the 18th the Regiment was posted on the banks of the Appomatox river, directly in front of the Rebel intrenchments. Their line extended for a long distance at nearly right angles with the river.

The position of the Regiment was a peculiar one. The bank of the river was forty or fifty feet above the water, and quite steep; and we were on this bank, entirely hidden from the Rebel works. The level ground above could be entirely swept by the enemy's guns. A charge was ordered, and in attempting to obey, the Regiment was obliged to get upon this ground, and the left was forced to swing around to the right to bring the whole line parallel to the enemy's works. When the order was

Another charge.

given this was attempted, but hardly had the men reached the level ground above when a line of men arose from behind the enemy's breastworks and poured in such a volley, that in an instant our line was cut down like grass, and the ground was covered with wounded men.

1864.

Disaster.

The enemy's fire was incessant, and nothing human could stand against it, so we fell back to our first position on the river bank. This attempt to charge the enemy's works resulted in a loss to the Regiment of six killed, and one officer (Captain Tucker) and twelve men wounded. Private Delany of Company A was killed, and E. B. Fairbanks and one other wounded.

On the 19th we were relieved by the Sixth Corps and started for Bermuda Hundred, bivouacked one night, and reached our destination at 10 A. M. of the 20th. We rested one day and one night, and then marched back to our old intrenchments. We were now in the trenches before Petersburg, being alternately two days on duty and two days in the camp at the rear. The Regiment had but one hundred and twenty-five men, including five officers. Companies A, C and K were now consolidated.

Useless march.

1864. The camp spoken of was situated in a ravine about half a mile from the works, and although at this distance, it was commanded by the enemy's guns. A small stream of water ran through this ravine, which afforded the boys the luxury of a bath.

At this time Company A numbered twenty-six men and no officers. Soldiers were returning to the Company from time to time, so the number varied daily.

This kind of life was wearing to the men, firing going on constantly, night and day. On the 30th of June, in the afternoon, we commenced shelling the enemy, and about 5 P. M. they replied. For an hour we had the heaviest cannonading we had ever experienced, and yet the Regiment, being behind the earthworks, had only five men wounded, and, singular as it may seem, all these by a single shot. These men were grouped together, and the shot *Effect of* struck right in the midst of them; one man had his *one shot.* foot taken off, another had a leg broken, a third was hit in the head, a fourth had both legs mangled, and the fifth received a slight contusion on his side. The ball could not be found. The men were taken to the hospital, and in amputating the leg of one of them—Private Thayer of Company D—the ball was actually discovered in his thigh, and proved to be a three pound shell.

1864.

July 4th, Lieutenant John W. Davis of Company C, wishing to have a moment's conversation with the Orderly Sergeant of Company A, advanced for that purpose in a stooping position to avoid the observation of the enemy. After having passed a few words of greeting, he unconsciously raised himself. It was but for a moment, yet on the instant a bullet struck him in the left shoulder, passing clean through his body, and lodged in the ground some rods to the rear. He placed his hand to his shoulder and exclaimed: "Sergeant, I'm a dead man," and fell to the ground. A stretcher was called and he was taken to the hospital tent. Lieutenant Davis survived this wound two years. He was a citizen of Worcester, and was for some time connected with the police force. He died August 2d, 1866, much regretted by those whose good fortune it was to be acquainted with him.

Lieut. Davis wounded.

While in another portion of the trenches nearer the enemy's line, a soldier was one day fatally shot in the head, and for a while our men were puzzled to know where the shot came from. Finally a soldier seated himself in the exact spot the wounded

1864.

man occupied when he was struck, and he noticed a large pine tree in the enemy's works. Watching he saw a puff of smoke come from the top of the tree, followed by the report of a rifle, so he concluded that a Rebel sharpshooter was concealed there. Several of our sharpshooters were called, and at a given signal all fired into the tree; a man was seen to fall from its branches, and we were troubled no more by shots from that quarter.

Explosive bullets.

Some talk there was of "Explosive Bullets," but I do not remember seeing one while in the service. A member of Company A found near Williamsburg (I think) a bullet about three inches long, having three blades which were intended to spread open as the bullet left the gun. It was a barbarous-looking affair, but this was the only one we ever saw.

Bullet-proof vests.

Bullet-proof vests were talked about to some extent. These consisted of two thin pieces of steel made to fit the body, which were to be worn one on either side and the cloth vest buttoned over them, as we were told. I never knew of any being used in this way, and I never saw but one. In this instance a soldier was cooking his "sublime flapjacks" in one of the sections. Truly, everything is of some use.

It has been estimated the entire length of the line of earthworks around Petersburg was over one hundred miles. These works included thirty-six forts (some with bastions), and over fifty batteries. The main line consisted chiefly of solid banks of earth, high enough to shield the men as they stood behind them, and too thick to be easily battered down with cannon. Forts and batteries were built along the line at convenient distances, and on rising ground when possible. Some of the forts before Petersburg were very large, and were furnished with bomb proofs. These were usually constructed of logs, six or eight feet high, and both top and sides were so covered with earth as to be impenetrable by shot or shell. The bomb proof at Fort Wadsworth was one hundred and fifty feet long and twelve feet wide. Some of these forts were fine specimens of military workmanship; for instance, Forts Fisher, Wadsworth and Sedgwick. Men with bold, brave hearts were required to attack and defend such places, but it was continually being done before Petersburg.

At Fort Stedman the distance between the Union and Rebel lines was scarcely six hundred feet. Between these were two picket lines—Union and

1864.

Works around Petersburg.

1864.

Rebel—two hundred feet apart. The men in these picket lines were in rifle pits, each of which contained two or three men; and night and day, in sun and rain, heat and cold, the men passed the weary hours in never-tiring vigilance, knowing that upon them might depend the fate of an army. The only protection for the men in the rifle pits was the small mound of loose earth thrown up in front of each, behind which they must keep entirely concealed.

Siege of Petersburg.

From the Appomatox river to Fort Sedgwick, a distance of perhaps four miles, firing was kept up, day and night, for months; and it was here that the Twenty-fifth Regiment was posted all the time it was in the trenches. Forts Sedgwick and Stedman were known among the soldiers as particularly "hot places." The former received the name of "Fort Hell"; and its opposite in the Rebel works—Fort Mahone—was called "Fort Damnation."

Probably there was more firing at the above mentioned forts than at any other place in the whole line. The battles around Petersburg may well be called the Waterloo of America, compared with which the Belgian Waterloo sinks into insignificance. The assault on Petersburg, June 15th, resulted in a loss to the Union troops of over ten thousand men. The actual siege of Petersburg began June 19th, 1864, and the place was not captured until April 3d, 1865—a period of nearly ten months.

The summer of 1864 was very dry, and there was much sickness among the troops, dysentery being the prevailing disease. We suffered more from heat this summer than ever before. There was no great variety in our rations while in the trenches; for instance, we had coffee and hard-tack for breakfast, boiled pork and hard-tack for dinner, coffee and hard-tack for supper. This diet month after month, together with the extremely hot weather, probably caused most of the sickness. We received at one time provisions from the Sanitary Commission, consisting of vegetables, pickles, canned fruit, condensed milk, etc. These things were a perfect godsend to the soldiers; and although the quantity, when divided among a regiment, was a small allowance to each man, still it did a great deal of good, and was thankfully received.

A short distance from our camp, on a slight elevation, our people had planted a big gun, which was fired every fifteen minutes, night and day, and sent a shell weighing one hundred pounds into

Margin notes: 1864. Disease. Rations. Sanitary Commission.

Petersburg every time. This gun was called the "Petersburg Express," and for some time was fired with great regularity.

While in the trenches the practice of exchanging newspapers with the enemy was started.* This was usually done in the morning, and in the following manner. One of our men would make known to the enemy that he wanted to exchange a paper by shouting: "Hello, Johnny." "Hello, Yank," was the reply. "Got any tobacco?" "Yes; got any papers?" "Yes; all right, Johnny, let's change." Our man would then wave a paper upon a ramrod until it was seen by the enemy, and they would wave one over their works in the same manner. Word was sent along the lines at the same time that no shots were to be fired. Our man would boldly raise himself head and shoulders above the works, and the enemy would do the same; both would then jump over the works and advance until they met half way between the lines. Here they would shake hands, exchange papers or coffee and tobacco, say

---

*In this exchange business the Johnnies usually wanted papers, coffee, and gum blankets, while the Yankees wanted papers and tobacco. We often got through this source news of battles fought before we heard of them from home. Frequently pieces that would give important information were cut out by both parties before the papers were exchanged.

a few friendly words, and then return to their respective lines. I never knew a shot fired from either side while this was going on. An instant after it would have been death if either had showed his head above the works.

1864.

July 22d Company A was reduced to its lowest number, and at this time might be said to have ceased to exist as an organization. One sergeant, one corporal, and three privates—five men all told, and not an officer left. For a time roll calls were dispensed with, as there were none to answer. Poor old Company A!

The Company reduced.

Up to this time there had been little or no rain, but we now had a heavy storm, and we got the full benefit of it, as the pits and trenches were filled with mud and water. The boys were obliged to stay there night and day, and sleep as best they could.

A storm.

The Regiment at this time was under command of Captain Parkhurst, and had dwindled down to four small companies, with five officers and less than one hundred guns.

During July the firing on each side was much less than when we first occupied the fortifications. It seemed as if both parties had become tired of the constant shooting at one another, and sometimes

1864. —— days would pass with scarcely any firing. The time dragged slowly away, and the monotony of the thing was hardly endurable.

At dark on the 29th of July we were relieved from the trenches, and at midnight, with sixty rounds of ammunition and three days' rations, we marched to the left a couple of miles, and reached the position occupied by the Ninth Corps. Here we lay on the ground until about 5 A. M., when a dull, heavy report startled us; this was accompanied *July 30.* by a shaking of the ground, and at the same instant *The Mine explosion.* our artillery all along the line began to play upon the enemy's works. The first report was the blowing up of a Rebel fort which had been undermined by our troops. This fort contained, as was reported, a regiment of Rebel infantry and sixteen guns. The Forty-eighth Pennsylvania regiment, under command of Lieutenant-Colonel Pleasants, originated and executed the plan of mining and blowing up the Rebel battery. The work was commenced June 25th, and completed in about a month. The distance was over five hundred feet. On the 27th of July the powder was placed in the mine, the whole charge consisting of three hundred and twenty kegs of twenty-five pounds each—in all, eight thousand pounds. The train was fired on the 30th of July, about 5 A. M. It was a terrible success. The crater made by the explosion was about two hundred and fifty feet long, fifty feet wide, and twenty-five feet deep.

Although we stood ready for action we were not in position to see the full effect of the explosion, but those who did, say it was a terrible sight—men, guns, timbers and earth going heavenward together. After a tedious delay the Ninth Corps charged, and carried a portion of the enemy's works, penetrating beyond the second line of intrenchments; but owing to some unaccountable misunderstanding, troops were not ordered to their support. The Rebels rallied, our boys were driven back, and it ended in the enemy regaining all the ground they had lost, including the blown-up fort.

After the explosion.

We left the scene of the explosion about noon of the 30th, and went again into the trenches, but not where we were previously. In our new situation the lines were very near together, and a sap had been run from our works and a short line established to within fifty or sixty feet of the Rebel lines. On looking through our loop holes we frequently saw the Rebels looking at us through theirs; and a rifle

—— barrel would often be introduced into these apertures in the endeavor to obtain a shot.

1864.

August 1st an arrangement was made under flag of truce, and parties were sent out to bury the dead from both colored and white regiments; the black burying the black, the white burying the white. This truce lasted from 6 to 11 A. M.

Truce for burial.

In our immediate front the enemy displayed a white flag, and a truce took place between our regiment and the troops of the enemy directly opposed to us. This was done because the lines were so near together that both parties feared to show themselves under the general truce. Each party in the meanwhile mounted their respective breastworks, and cooly sat gazing upon the other and talking like old friends. The distance was so short that small shells with fuse lighted had been thrown from one line to the other, after the manner of hand grenades.

A good deal of fun passed between us and the Johnnies, and some twitting upon facts. One Union boy asked a Rebel: "How did you like that style of going to heaven, Johnny?" referring to the explosion. "We rather gave you hell that time, didn't we?" said another. But the talk for the most part was good natured; and the burial of the dead went on. This was dreadful business; the bodies had lain upon the ground since the day of the explosion, and had been exposed to the hot sun during the day and to the dampness at night, so that their condition was horrible. Pits were dug and the bodies thrown in any way. When the work was completed a signal gun was fired, and the troops hurried back to their respective intrenchments.

The Twenty-fifth Regiment was relieved by the Twenty-third Massachusetts on the fifth of August, and we had fallen back to our old camp, when, about 6 P. M., we were startled by a sudden explosion followed by volleys of musketry, while our batteries opened fire. We quickly fell into line and marched to the scene of the trouble, and found that the enemy had attempted to mine that portion of the works we had just left. We had expected this, for we had heard the Rebels at work digging for some time previously. They must have miscalculated the distance, for the explosion took place just outside of our line, and consequently did no harm, with the exception of overthrowing a few gabions and burying for a few minutes some half a dozen of our men. The plucky Twenty-third held the line.

1864.

Counter-mining.

1864. Several men were wounded by the Rebel guns which commenced firing as soon as the explosion occurred, and Colonel Stedman, who commanded our brigade, was killed. At this time troops had been taken from our line and sent elsewhere, and the duty was now more severe than ever, as we were in the trenches four successive days, with only two of relief.

A few days after this explosion we occupied another position in the intrenchments where the lines were about two hundred feet apart, and between them for a long distance was a great field of corn. When the fortifications were built this corn was some two feet high, while at this time it was six feet in height, and fairly concealed the Rebel works from our view. One dark night, after the moon had gone down, men were sent over the breastworks to cut down this corn, which was quickly and quietly accomplished as far as could be done, and the next day the boys were feasting on the green ears.

Green corn.

One night a big fire was seen in Petersburg. We could hear the bells ring and the engines whistle, while our big gun, "The Petersburg Express," sent its regular messages into that afflicted city.

While lying in the trenches in the vicinity of Fort Stedman, a large gun in the enemy's line had caused us a great deal of trouble. One day a large mortar was put in position and trained upon this gun. The soldiers crowded around to witness the effect of the first shell. In a few minutes it was fired, and its course was watched with a great deal of interest; it was seen to strike outside the enemy's works and harmlessly explode. A second shell was fired. Higher and higher it ascended and soon began falling in a graceful curve in the exact range of the big gun. It was seen to fall inside the enemy's works, and an instant later exploded; a cloud of dust was thrown high in the air, in which could be seen the form of a man, pieces of timber, etc. This shell had done its work, and the Rebel gun was dismounted.

1864.

A Rebel gun silenced.

One day we had an exceedingly heavy rain, and the little stream which ran through the ravine where we camped suddenly overflowed its banks, and rushed along, a perfect torrent, filling the whole ravine with water. So suddenly did this take place that some sick soldiers lying in their tents were near being drowned. Large army wagons were carried down the stream for some distance, which

A torrent.

1864. shows the strength of the torrent. The waters subsided as quickly as they had risen; no lives were lost and little damage was done.

At this time the Regiment was receiving recruits from Massachusetts, and such god-forsaken specimens as some of them were, it would be hard to match. It seemed as if the good, patriotic people of Worcester had robbed hospitals to find substitutes to fill their quota. There were old, broken-down men, very young boys; and one or more were idiotic *Tough recruits.* and one was afflicted with epilepsy. Several were so lame that they had to carry canes, and taken altogether they were the toughest lot of recruits the Regiment had received. These men had taken their bounties, and one of them actually received more money ($1200) than any individual of the original members did for three years' service. The majority of these recruits were returned as being unfit for duty, but the persons for whom they were enrolled as substitutes, and by whom they were paid for this *non*-service, effectually escaped thereby their liability to the draft.

August 27th found the Regiment in camp near Cobb's Hill, where it had been sent for a much needed, often promised, and well earned rest. If we reckon the time from April 26th, when the Regiment was assigned to Heckman's Brigade, until this date, August 27th, we have four months, during which we were constantly on duty and actually under fire. This camp was a comfortable one, and it was a treat to be able to walk about without fear of being shot. The lines at this point were a quarter of a mile apart, and the Union and Rebel pickets were on very friendly terms, exchanging papers and conversing with each other daily. The Rebel pickets even saluted our officers when they chanced to see them.

1864.

A rest.

About September 1st orders were received for the Regiment to start for North Carolina, so we sailed down the James again, to Portsmouth, where we obtained our knapsacks left there four months before. On September 6th we went on board the steamer *Wenonah*, and proceeded on our way, but a thick fog came on, and we anchored for the night near the village of Hampton. A heavy gale blowing outside detained us for a time, but at length we sailed from Hampton Roads, and after a fair passage around Cape Hatteras, arrived at New Berne on the 10th.

Off for North Carolina.

1864.

New Berne again.

Our camp was pitched on the bank of the Trent river, opposite the town and near the railroad bridge which was destroyed when New Berne was captured. Most of the companies were sent out on picket duty. It was amusing to observe the boys as they wandered around the camp, careless and happy,—no firing here, no being shot at; and the time of service was drawing to a close for the "Used-to-bes."

Yellow fever.

At this time a strange disease broke out in New Berne which proved generally fatal. This was at last pronounced to be yellow fever, and it continued to increase in virulence until it became epidemic. The people died in such numbers that it was almost impossible to bury them. Thirteen hundred died in six weeks. Comrade George F. Penniman died September 18th, and Comrade Reuben H. DeLuce on the 20th, both of yellow fever. These men had been detailed from our company, and had remained on duty in New Berne ever since its capture, escaping all the hardships of the campaign to die as time drew near for them to be discharged from service. During the prevalence of this disease in New Berne many sad cases came to our knowledge; in one instance a house was broken open by the police and a whole family found dead; yet many of the sick recovered. The disease was accounted for by the filthy condition of the town.

1864.

We visited our old home, Camp Oliver, and found the ground covered with negro shanties. One or two old cook houses were the only signs remaining of the occupation of the place by the Twenty-fifth.

On the 5th of October those of the Regiment who had not re-enlisted—fifteen officers and two hundred and forty-eight men—bade their comrades "Goodbye," and, under command of Captain Denny, took the cars for Morehead City. We were bound for *home* now, and not for the battle field. At Morehead City we went on board the steamer, *Dudley Buck*, and putting out to sea, doubled Cape Hatteras once more (the sixth time for some of us), reaching Fortress Monroe at 10 A. M. of October 7th. On account of coming from a port infected with yellow fever we anchored at the quarantine ground. After some delay here, we were allowed to proceed to New York, where we arrived on Sunday, the 9th. While on the passage from North Carolina two men (not of the 25th) had died of yellow fever, and were buried at sea. We were held in quarantine until Wednesday, the 12th, when we passed up to the

Homeward bound.

city and disembarked. That afternoon the Regiment took passage on one of the Norwich line of boats for New London, reaching that place sometime after midnight. Here a delay was proposed, as our Worcester friends wished to give us a public reception on our arrival; but the boys were impatient to see home, and, taking the regular train, we reached our journey's end at 4 A. M. of October 13th.

What a contrast to that October day of three years before. Then it was a bright and beautiful day, with thousands to bid us good-bye; now it was a cold and cheerless morning, and (not being expected at that early hour) none to give us welcome. But it was soon noised abroad, and the City Hall was filled with people eager to get a sight of the soldiers. Among the first to greet us was "Our Old Captain," Colonel Pickett, still suffering from his wound of June 3d at Cold Harbor; and lame as he was, he had walked to the City Hall to bid his old comrades welcome—and what a greeting was that! After a collation provided by the City, we were addressed by the Mayor, Hon. D. Waldo Lincoln, Colonel William S. Lincoln (of the 34th), and Colonel Pickett. We were then dismissed to meet again October 20th for final muster-out.

On our departure from New Berne those of the Regiment who had re-enlisted—three hundred and sixty men—were consolidated into four companies, with ten officers. They did picket and guard duty around New Berne, and participated in an expedition to Kinston and a brilliant engagement near Wise's Forks, N. C. This portion of the Regiment was mustered out July 21st, 1865—after the close of the war.

1864.

On the 20th of October, 1864, the Company met again in Worcester, and, in front of the Old City Hall, were mustered out of the service of the United States. The original Company A, Twenty-fifth Regiment Massachusetts Volunteers was no more. Our full term of service—three years—had expired—long years they had been to us; and with the proud satisfaction that duty to our country had been "well done," we found ourselves again private citizens.

Oct. 20. Mustered out.

With hand-shaking, tearful eyes, and every expression of good will and farewell toward each other, the members of the Company separated, never to meet again; never again to rally under the starry splendors of "Old Glory"; never again to participate in the wild excitement of the charge, or with quick

—— eye and elastic step find place in the skirmish line; but henceforth to the end to lead the quiet life of peaceful citizens.

Company A Association was formed some years later, and annual reunions have been regularly held; but the men who were mustered out on that 20th of October, 1864, never all met again, for—

> "Some are dead, and some are gone,
> And some are scattered and alone."

One by one they disappear—drifting away like withered leaves, on the uncertain tide of later years.

At present writing about thirty members of the Company Association come together at the annual meetings.

———

And now, kind, indulgent comrades, farewell. The story is ended. Would it were better told, but "what is written, is written."

If any shall find pleasure in following through these pages—the wanderings of this band of men, this company of soldiers; shall glory with them in their victories, and sympathize with them in their losses and reverses; if any comrade shall call up pleasant memories of his soldier life by the perusal of this simple narrative—then, possibly, this story has not been told in vain.

Again, farewell,

SAMUEL H. PUTNAM,

Late Orderly Sergeant, Company A, and Sergeant Major, 25th Regiment, Mass. Vols.

Worcester, Mass., April 30, 1886.

THE DEAD OF COMPANY A.

₊ Names of those who died in the Service.

GEORGE E. CURTIS, died at Hatteras Inlet, N. C., Jan. 21, 1862.
ELI PIKE, killed at New Berne, March 15, 1862.
LUCIUS F. KINGMAN, died at New Berne, Sept. 24, 1862.
EDWIN D. WATERS, died at New Berne, Nov. 5, 1862.
JOHN B. SAVAGE, died a prisoner at Richmond, March 1, 1864.
WILLIAM E. HOLMAN, killed at Proctor's Creek, May 12, 1864.
HENRY GOULDING, killed at Drewry's Bluff, May 14, 1864.
LYMAN J. PRENTISS, died of wounds at Hampton Hospital, May 16, 1864.
WALTER H. RICHARDS, died of wounds at Richmond, May 18, '64.
FRANCIS B. BROCK, killed at Cold Harbor, June 3, 1864.

—— IRA LINDSEY, killed at Cold Harbor, June 3, 1864.
SIDNEY J. ATKINSON, killed at Cold Harbor, June 3, 1864.
LIBERTY W. STONE, died of wounds at Milford, Mass., July 5, '64.
JOSEPH L. DELANEY, killed at Petersburg, June 8, 1864.
JAMES WHITE, died of wounds in New York harbor, June 23, 1864.
ABEL S. ANGELL, died June 28, 1864.
BENJAMIN C. GREENE, shot by Rebel guard while sitting on a window sill at Libby Prison; died of the wound, Sept. 11, '64.
GEORGE F. PENNIMAN, died of yellow fever at New Berne, Sept. 18, 1864.
REUBEN H. DELUCE, died of yellow fever at New Berne, Sept. 20, 1864.
JEROME H. FULLER, died a prisoner at Florence, S. C., Oct. 26, '64.
JOHN A. THOMPSON, died at New Berne, 1864.
JAMES M. HERVEY, died in New Berne, 1864.

www.ingramcontent.com/pod-product-compliance
Lightning Source LLC
Chambersburg PA
CBHW030004240426
43672CB00007B/816